# Play Golf
# the Pebble Beach Way

*Lose Five Strokes
Without Changing Your Swing*

**Laird Small with Dave Allen**

TRIUMPH
B O O K S

Triumph Books and colophon are registered trademarks of Random House, Inc.

Pebble Beach, Pebble Beach Golf Links, Pebble Beach Golf Academy™, The Lodge at Pebble Beach™, The Beach and Tennis Club™, Spyglass Hill Golf Course, Stillwater Cove, 17-Mile Drive, The Lone Cypress™, The Heritage Logo, and their respective images are trademarks, service marks, and trade dress of Pebble Beach Company. Used under license.

Library of Congress Copyright-in-Publication Data

Small, Laird.
  Play golf the Pebble Beach way : lose five strokes without changing your swing / Laird Small with Dave Allen.
     p. cm.
  ISBN 978-1-60078-329-6
  1. Golf—Training.  2. Swing (Golf)  3. Pebble Beach Golf Links (Pebble Beach, Calif.)
I. Allen, Dave, 1968–  II. Title.
  GV979.T68S63 2010
  796.352—dc22
                            2010007696

Published by:
  **Triumph Books**
  542 South Dearborn Street
  Suite 750
  Chicago, Illinois 60605
  (312) 939-3330
  Fax (312) 663-3557
  www.triumphbooks.com

Printed in U.S.A.
ISBN: 978-1-60078-329-6
Designed by Patricia Frey
Photographs by Fred Vuich except as otherwise indicated

# Contents

# Foreword

I'm truly one of the luckiest sports fans on Earth. Each year, CBS entrusts me to broadcast such noteworthy events as the Masters, NCAA Men's Final Four, and AFC Championship Game, even the Super Bowl every three years. How's that for a dream foursome?

As honored as I am to call these events—and I have to say that broadcasting 25 consecutive Masters tournaments has been the single greatest achievement of my career—there is no more enjoyable week year in and year out than Pebble Beach AT&T week. It's not the most challenging or rewarding, but it's the most fun. Walking around the storied links, you feel the presence of Bing Crosby and his happy band of revelers, and the comfort with which the celebrities mingle with the crowd is something you don't see anywhere else. You can sense the history, too. I have stored in my brain all of the famous golf moments that have taken place at Pebble Beach, whether it be Jack Nicklaus' 1-iron into the 17th green at the 1972 U.S. Open, or Tiger Woods holing his second shot from the 15th fairway and coming back from seven down with seven to play against Matt Gogel in 2000.

There is also a spirituality about Pebble Beach that is different from any other place I've ever been, and from the very first moment I stepped on this sacred sod as a 10-year-old, I could feel it. Nowhere is this sense of spirituality greater than on the otherworldly par-3 7th hole. For most of the 25 years I've been coming to the AT&T Pebble Beach National Pro-Am for CBS, I have made it a point to get up before dawn, walk down the 18th hole, take the dogleg at the 17th and 4th tees, and lightly jog out to the 7th hole. When I finally reach the hole, which sits atop a bluff overlooking Stillwater Cove, I stand along the picket fence behind the tee box and wait for daybreak.

It's a very prayerful, retrospective place for me. On the first day I jog there, I take inventory of the blessings in my life and the good fortune that has come my way since the last time I was at this very special place. I give thanks for having a chance to be back at Pebble Beach again, and I always think about my dad and the time we played a round together here the day after the 1990 Pro-Am. It was my dad, after all, who introduced me to this heavenly spot back in 1969.

February 2009 was my first time back to the 7th tee since my dad passed away the previous June, and as I performed my usual routine, the sun suddenly shot up above the San Lucia

Mountains off to the east. I closed my eyes for a minute, and when I reopened them, I found myself standing underneath a huge rainbow. One end of the rainbow was over the Pacific Ocean, and the other end of the arch was right over my head. People always say when you lose a loved one, they send you a message back that everything is okay. I really felt as if that's what this was. It was truly powerful.

The message in Laird Small's book, *Play Golf the Pebble Beach Way*, is also a very convincing one. The lesson is simple: You don't get better by constantly tinkering with your swing or trying out all the latest tips in the golf magazines; you drop strokes by learning how to play the game. You can't do that sitting in front of a monitor watching a video analysis of your swing; you've got to learn how to perform under pressure and take your game from the range to the course.

I received very little instruction when I was a kid, yet I was still good enough to make the University of Houston golf team. My level of play began to slip, however, when I got to Houston, partly because I was intimidated by my teammates. They had much bigger résumés and picture-perfect golf swings. I didn't improve, I just flattened out, and that's when I began to pursue my real love of sports broadcasting.

In recent years, I have lost much of the feel for playing the game that I had as a kid. In many ways, I too have been a victim of the glut of instruction that is out there; there's too much data in the computer. It's a lot more fun when you play with feel, because you open up your senses and swing with much more freedom. You're not constantly overloading on swing thoughts.

Most amateurs today try to be so exact with their swings that they forget they're playing a game. My goodness, isn't that what it's all about? We're supposed to take in the sights, the senses, and the sounds of all these places we're fortunate enough to play. Wouldn't it be fun to play Pebble Beach without being consumed by the thought of swing angles and grip pressures? These are things I never thought of as a kid, and sometimes I could shoot par golf or even better.

*Play Golf the Pebble Beach Way* will teach you how to play with feel, instead of how to overthink. It will help you overcome your first-tee jitters and fear of hazards and propel you to hit more greens without changing anything in your swing. Technique is important but so is being able to plan for your shot tendencies and knowing how to bounce back after a tough hole. You can't help but play better and enjoy the game more after reading this book. I know I have.

—Jim Nantz, CBS Sports commentator and author of *Always by My Side*

# Acknowledgments

**M**y most sincere thanks to Dave Allen, who transformed my ideas into legible English. Thank you for your patience over the several years it took to get this project completed. And Lorin Anderson, who along with Dave knew this was a good idea and never gave up on the concept. Thank you for finding Marilyn Allen to help put all the right people in place and orchestrate the book. A special thanks to Mitch Rogatz at Triumph Books for believing in the book and its premise. Thanks also to Triumph Books managing editor Don Gulbrandsen for his work on the project. Fred Vuich: Your artistry is truly amazing; thank you for helping to bring my words to life with your photography. Thanks to Martin Miller and Robert Brown for your hole-by-hole diagrams of the course in Chapter 11; they add a wonderful touch to the book.

My sincerest appreciation to Pebble Beach Company for their trust and belief in me over these past 22 years and counting. To RJ Harper, thank you for supporting the work and pushing me forward; your encouragement means a great deal. Special thanks to David Stivers for his vision on how this book fits into the Pebble Beach brand, and Neal Hotelling, whose knowledge and appreciation for Pebble Beach history made me realize that this project was possible. To Bill Perocchi and Cody Plott, thank you for the green light and all of your support behind the book.

I want to thank Paul Spengler for jumping in with both feet and being so excited and willing to help at every turn. Your enthusiasm for life and the game of golf and your ability to grow relationships are things I've come to truly admire. Thank you and Pebble Beach Company for drilling into me the desire to "exceed the expectations of every guest every time."

My deepest gratitude to Steve McLennan, who gave me a chance by hiring me as the head professional at Spyglass Hill. How did you know it would lead to this?

A special thank you to Arnold Palmer, Tom Kite, Tom Watson, Jack Nicklaus, Kirk Triplett, Bobby Clampett, and Johnny Miller for sharing their stories about Pebble Beach and how they played the game. Your words of wisdom will help golfers at every turn for years to come.

I would not have been able to write this book without the help of so many wonderful people and teaching professionals who have shared their time, ideas, and spirit for the game with me over the years. To Jim Flick (Coach), you took me under your wing and taught me how to teach the game. I appreciate all you have shared with me and how you continue to do so. To John Geertsen Sr., thank you for teaching a young boy how to swing the club and play the game. You were a wonderful role model. To Ben Doyle, thank you for sharing the laws and principles of The Golfing Machine and always walking with grace. To Doug Hofer, Paul Runyan, Bob Toski, Rick Martino, Jim Hardy, Carol Mann, Dan Pasquariello, Jim Hayes, Katherine Marren, Tommy Masters, Eric Alpenfels, Paul Schempp, Mike Malaska, Mike Bender, Chuck Cook, Patrick Kennedy, Bill Brown, Gary Knapp, Bob Gregg, and John "Gee" White of Heart Math: You have all taught me that it's the individual who counts and that we teach people, not methods. Your input has been thoughtful, insightful, and always honest. Thank you!

Many thanks to Garry Lester and Fred Shoemaker for sharing the art of the possible; you've encouraged me to look at different ways to become a coach and teacher of the game, one that respects the perfect learner that we all are. To Glen Albaugh, David Cook, and Fran Pirozollo for helping me to unravel how to transfer the skill from the range to the course, and Ingrid Gudenas and Drew Johnson for sharing your ideas on learning and proficiency and the writings of L. Ron Hubbard, truly revolutionary ideas that will help golfers play and learn the game much faster. To Frank Quattrone: Thank you for pushing me to get it DONE!

Jim Nantz, thank you for your friendship and the wonderful foreword to this book.

To my dear friend, Tom Sullivan, whose wonderful spirit and courage is with me every single day: Thank you for all of your ideas, help, and friendship. You are truly inspiring!

All the people above have been instrumental in this project and my life, and for that I am blessed. A special thank you to my mom, Alice Jean, and my grandparents; they put me out on the golf course and supported my intention and desire to become a golf professional.

To Honor, my wife and life partner, along with our boys Riley and Emmett: Thank you for the daily inspiration, joy, laughter, and love. You are keeping up your end of the deal!

# Introduction

Research conducted by the National Golf Foundation (NGF) shows that the average score for all golfers on an 18-hole regulation course is 100; 97 for men and 114 for women. That average has changed little over the years, despite advances in equipment that have allowed us to hit a ball farther and straighter than ever before. So why aren't golfers improving?

The excuses range from less practice time to longer, more difficult course designs to an overabundance of instruction (paralysis by analysis). Sure, all of these things play a factor, but the biggest reason golfers don't improve is because they spend too little time learning how to play the game. They don't know how to take the skills they've learned and apply them on the golf course, when the shots really matter.

*Playing the game* means understanding your shot tendencies and accurately predicting what the ball is going to do after you hit it. It's knowing what your tendencies are under pressure and being able to plan for them. It's not about changing your swing midround or trying out the latest Band-Aid—it's about playing smart with the swing you already have.

In *Play Golf the Pebble Beach Way*, Laird Small, director of the Pebble Beach Golf Academy, walks you through all 18 holes of the famous course, just as if he was on your bag. In the process, he teaches you how to pull the right club for your approach shot, manage your first-tee jitters, read sticky lies, think like a pro, and bounce back from a bad hole. Drawing on his many years of experience as a caddie and now as an instructor at Pebble Beach, Small demonstrates how to play the game and score better by changing your mental approach to golf—not your mechanics.

The 2003 PGA Teacher of the Year, Small shares anecdotes and lessons he learned from some of the greatest champions in golf—including Jack Nicklaus, Tom Watson, Arnold Palmer, Johnny Miller, Tom Kite, and Tiger Woods—and how they navigated their way around this storied course. From Nicklaus' famous 1-iron to the 17th green at the 1972 U.S. Open to Watson's remarkable chip-in on the same hole 10 years later, you'll hear how these legends pulled off each shot and what they were thinking.

In addition, you'll learn Nicklaus' and Palmer's secrets to bouncing back, Watson's thoughts on overcoming fear, Kite's essentials for solid wedge play, and Miller's take on attacking the green and playing the par-3s.

By the time you're done reading this book, you'll not only be ready to play Pebble Beach, you'll have the tools necessary to shoot your lowest scores ever, no matter where you are. You'll be able to transfer what you learned in this book to your own course and your own game, and you won't have to wade through hundreds of complicated terms and swing details. You'll play better golf and have more fun doing so.

—Dave Allen

# Play Golf
## the Pebble Beach Way

The par-4 1st hole at Pebble Beach, a slight dogleg to the right.

# Chapter 1

# How to Beat the First-Tee Jitters

I n the storied history of the AT&T Pebble Beach National Pro-Am, it's often referred to as the hotel-in-one. Fighting to make the Sunday cut in the pro-am for the first time ever, actor Jack Lemmon sliced his tee shot on the 1st hole into an adjacent room at The Lodge.

"Honey, I'm home," Lemmon joked upon muffing the shot.

Turns out he was home. The ball actually found its way into the first-floor room where he and his wife, Felicia, were staying.

Another year, Lemmon nearly whiffed on his opening tee shot at Cypress Point and floated the ball into the hands of a woman in the gallery. His longtime playing partner, Peter Jacobsen, immediately asked the woman to throw the ball down the fairway before Lemmon would notice where the ball went.

Perhaps no golfer epitomizes the struggles of the first tee more than Lemmon, who once said he'd trade an Oscar for the chance to play on Sunday in the pro-am at Pebble Beach. It never happened. Lemmon, who passed away in 2001, missed the cut in all 25 of his pro-am appearances, 16 with Jacobsen. He came closest to fulfilling his dream in 1998, when he and Jacobsen were 16-under par heading into Saturday's play, only to have the pro-am canceled that weekend due to inclement weather.

# Beating the First-Tee Jitters

**1. Deflect the Outcome:** Embrace the NATO (*N*ot *A*ttached *T*o *O*utcome) mindset, focusing on the present—not on what has occurred or what might happen.

**2. Forget Who's Watching:** There are fewer eyes watching than you think, and they're more concerned about their own shots than whether you top the ball or knock it down the center of the fairway.

**3. Find Your Quiet Zone:** Turn off the chatter in your head—all those verbal commands and negative thoughts—and discover peace and quiet "in the zone."

**4. Slow Down to Beat Tension:** Use a variety of "alternative" practice swings to overcome the effects of adrenaline and reduce your anxiousness on the tee.

**5. Take Your Range Swing to the First Tee:** Don't go to the range simply to practice; use the time to loosen up, develop rhythm, and work on your short game.

**6. Make a Full Rehearsal Swing:** Focus on making as tension-free a swing as possible and apply it to your real swing.

**7. Go on the Defensive:** Successful second shots start by selecting the right club off the tee—one that leaves you in the fairway and a reasonable distance from the hole.

Lemmon joked that he'd rather perform *Hamlet* unrehearsed than hit a tee shot in front of thousands of spectators. And that's how many golfers feel on the first tee. No shot in golf, with the possible exception of a forced carry over water or a testy, downhill three-foot putt, draws as many butterflies to your stomach as the first tee shot. Sensing that there are many eyes watching you, you don't want to be embarrassed by cold-topping it off the first tee. What makes the shot even more difficult are the expectations that golfers heap on it—i.e., stripe it down the middle, and you're thinking about opening with a birdie, but slice it out of bounds and you might as well head back to the car.

This chapter deals with these fears and expectations and teaches you how to cope with the first-tee jitters that plague even the most experienced of golfers.

## 1. Deflect the Outcome

When you step onto the first tee, it's not the friendliest of environments. As your eyes scan the fairway, you see bunkers, out-of-bounds stakes, sloped fairways, heavy rough—nothing but trouble. It's hard to see the fairway grass that lies in front of you. All of a sudden, you're thinking about all of the things that can go wrong, instead of those that can go right.

Your objective on the first tee, as with every shot in golf, is to not attach yourself to the outcome of the shot—i.e., everything that can go wrong with the shot. I use the acronym NATO (*N*ot *A*ttached *T*o *O*utcome) to describe this mind-set. You want to focus on the present, not what has occurred in the past ("The last time I was here, I drove it into the

**Actor and comedian Jack Lemmon once hit his opening tee shot into The Lodge, adjacent to the first tee at Pebble Beach.** William C. Brooks, PBC Archives

fairway bunker and made double bogey") or what might happen in the future ("What if I top it in front of all of these people?").

There are several things you can do to remove yourself from the outcome of the shot and stay committed to the present. You can create a mantra, or swing thought, designed to help you achieve a specific goal. For example, a lot of players on the PGA Tour focus simply on making solid contact—driving the middle of the clubface into the ball—off the tee. They know if they hit the ball solid, there's a fairly good chance it will wind up in the vicinity of

where they aimed. It's the mishits that drive them crazy. So they create an internal dialogue ("Start the club down slowly," "See the club hit the ball") or, in many cases, an external one, to help them achieve solid contact. Sam Snead used to hum a tune when he played, which encouraged him to swing in perfect rhythm and, thus, make solid contact.

Another way to deflect the outcome is to establish a reliable preshot routine. Get all of the rehearsal stuff out of the way behind the ball (choose your target, pick your club, envision the shape and trajectory of the shot), so when you cross the threshold—or line of commitment—you're done thinking about the swing and the possible outcomes of it. Stay committed to your intention and hit the ball. If you start to have doubts about your intention and any negative thoughts surface, take a step back from the ball and start over again.

The game of golf also affords us the opportunity to be aware of our surroundings while we're in the moment so that we can make a shift in our consciousness. For example, you might find you're one of only a few people out on the golf course one late afternoon. Sensing that no one is watching, you can free up your mind and body to really let loose, without any fear of consequences. Whatever allows you to shift your mind into the present state—whether it's humming a tune, looking at the outline of the trees in front of you, or pretending that you're hitting into the ocean—seize on it.

## 2. Forget Who's Watching

Making the task even more difficult on the first tee is the perception that everyone is watching you, from your fellow playing partners and the people in the pro shop to those waiting to tee off in the group behind you. The anxiety is even greater on famous courses like Pebble Beach Golf Links or St. Andrews because of their rich history and heavenly mystique.

The reality is, there are fewer eyes on you than you think, and they're more likely to be concerned about their own tee shot or second shot than whether or not you top it or knock it down the center of the fairway. If you crush your drive, you won't hear cheers or applause like you would at a PGA Tour event. You might get

a "nice shot" out of your playing partners, but you're certainly not going to hear them groan or laugh at you if you mishit it. Once again, it's important to focus on the shot at hand, not the outcome or what your playing partners might think of the outcome, because that's the last thing on their minds.

Besides, what's the worst thing that can happen? You pop it up off the tee? How long does that feeling last? It may stay with you for a few shots or holes but probably no longer than that. Now, what's the best thing that can happen? You stripe it down the middle past all of your playing partners? Again, how long does that feeling last? A few holes at most. If neither is too long, then why get emotional about the outcome, whether it's good or bad?

If you're playing with a total stranger or group of strangers, it might behoove you to unload your baggage on the first tee. Tell your group that you're nervous playing in front of strangers and that your only goal on the first tee is to make a tension-free swing. This way, you remove the outcome from the equation and you get rewarded on your ability to make a tension-free swing. You'll be complimented on your motion ("Boy, you made a really good swing on that!"), instead of the outcome. Chances are, if you make a smooth, tension-free swing, you'll also be rewarded with a good tee shot as well.

## 3. Find Your Quiet Zone

If you asked Annika Sorenstam, David Duval, Michael Jordan, or anyone who's ever been "in the zone," they would all tell you the same thing—how quiet it is. When most amateurs are playing poorly, their minds are full of chatter.

They're bombarded with verbal commands such as "keep your head down," "turn your hips," "shift your weight," or "keep your left arm straight." Plus, they carry all of these negative thoughts, which they have to combat with an equal amount or more of positive thoughts. The back and forth between the two and the internal conversation in their heads is loud and out of control.

When you're playing well, however, there's an absence of all this chatter. It's very quiet and peaceful. You're not thinking about outcomes; you're thinking about hitting the ball to your target. The next time you're on the first tee, see if you can get to this quiet place in your mind. If any negative thoughts surface, let them go. Don't react to them positively or negatively. As soon as you create a fight between negative and positive thoughts, there has to be an outcome.

## 4. Slow Down to Beat Tension

What makes golfers tight on the first tee isn't so much nerves as it is adrenaline. The release of this hormone stimulates the heart, increases your blood sugar and muscular strength, and generally makes you feel very anxious to get started. As a result, everything starts to speed up, which creates tension. You have to recognize this tension for what it is and slow it down before you become too jittery.

One way to do this is to take a few practice swings with a heavier-weighted club (such as a

**Swinging a heavier-weighted club, such as an 8-iron, will encourage you to slow down on the first tee.**

**Tom Watson used to beat tension by making a few practice swings with the club upside down. This gave him a better feel for the clubhead.**

pitching wedge or 8-iron) than the one you plan on using off the first tee. Swinging less club is a verbal cue to slow down. It also helps to take a few deep breaths before you swing, breathing in slowly through your nose and out through your mouth. Feel as though you're expanding your rib cage like a balloon as you breathe in. This will bring more air into your lungs, which helps to slow your heart rate.

Tom Watson used to beat tension on the tee with some unusual practice swings. He'd turn the club upside down, gripping that part of the shaft closest to the clubhead, and make several continuous swings with the handle pointed down toward the ground. Then he would turn the club around the correct way and swing normally. This gave him a greater feel for the weight of the clubhead, which

# Triplett: Immerse Yourself in the Process

You beat tension on the first tee just as you would with any other shot, by zeroing in on what you're trying to do, says two-time PGA Tour winner Kirk Triplett. "Have a picture of your target, be committed to your target, and know exactly how you're going to execute the shot," says Triplett.

"If you keep your mind occupied, you don't have time to think negatively," he added.

"Tension comes from thinking about the results of what's going to happen ('Am I going to skull this in the trees and look like a complete knucklehead?')," said Triplett. "If you think about what you're supposed to, there's no room for these kinds of thoughts."

Photo courtesy Getty Images

would appear much heavier when he turned it around to its normal position. Then, he would think about running the clubhead back into the ball squarely.

When your body is tight, you lose awareness of what you're trying to swing. Your grip pressure increases, your arms lock up, and your facial muscles tighten, which makes it very hard to feel the clubhead. This drill helps restore that feel.

A similar exercise is to hold the shaft vertically in front of you, so the weight of the club is distributed evenly throughout the shaft and the club feels very light. Next, lower the shaft until it's parallel to the ground. At this point, your hands and arms should feel much

heavier. You want the shaft somewhere in between—at a 45-degree angle to you—so you can feel the club balanced properly in your hands and the weight you're trying to swing. This exercise, made famous by Hall of Fame instructor Jim Flick, works much like the Watson drill in that it helps to restore your awareness of the clubhead.

## 5. How to Take Your Range Swing to the First Tee

One thing I hear all the time from my students is, "Laird, I hit the ball great on the range, but when I get to the first tee, it all falls apart." If you're having trouble transferring your success on the practice range to the first tee, you need to change the way you look at the practice range. Most amateurs hit the range with the intention of warming up and wind up practicing instead. Somewhere along the way, they hit two or three bad shots—or good ones—and they want to either get rid of the bad feel or ingrain the new one. Consequently, they spend the last few minutes prior to teeing off working on something mechanical in their swings.

The tour players proceed to the practice range with the same intention—to warm up—but they never lose that intention. They hit their clubs with the intention of getting loose and developing a good sense of rhythm and timing for each club, not with any orientation to the outcome of these shots. They want to take away the feeling of hitting the ball solidly. In addition, you'll see them go through their normal preshot routine and hit different clubs (and shots) to different targets. This way, when they go from the multiple-shot environment of the driving range to the single-shot environment of the course, they're much better prepared for the additional time required between shots.

Another thing you'll see the tour pros do that the amateurs typically don't is practice the short game. They'll spend at least half of their warm-up time putting, pitching, and chipping, whereas most amateurs will beat drivers and occasionally hit some putts before heading to the first tee. Spend a little more time on your short game as you warm up. You'll not only gain some confidence around the greens, but you'll get a better feel for the ball coming off the clubface, which transfers over to the tee. Besides, you'll be hitting the majority of

**On your rehearsal swing, try and make as free a swing as possible, then duplicate the same tension-free motion over the ball.**

# Tom Kite: Take Dead Aim

There's little you can do on the practice range to simulate the butterflies you feel in your stomach on the first tee, especially the first tee at Pebble Beach. It's a feeling you're not accustomed to, like giving a speech in front of a packed auditorium. The mistake amateurs make, says Tom Kite, is that they pay too much attention to this feeling, as opposed to what they're trying to do in the golf swing.

"It doesn't really matter how your stomach feels or whether your hands are shaking," said Kite. "It's all about making a golf swing and committing to the target."

Kite, who shares the course record at Pebble Beach (10-under-par 62) with David Duval, said he still has first-tee jitters, only he doesn't see them as a sign of weakness.

"It's a huge positive because all that adrenaline pumping through your body, that's what allows you to do super-human things," said Kite. "Your concentration gets better, your body becomes more athletic, more dynamic. You have to understand that it's a positive thing, not a negative, and when you start to realize that and look forward to the feeling of getting nervous, that's when it becomes an advantage."

Once you learn to accept these nerves, the only thing left to do, says Kite, is "take dead aim," something his legendary teacher, Harvey Penick, used to tell him before every shot.

"My interpretation of 'take dead aim' is that for the two or three seconds it takes to play a shot, you have to be so locked in that nothing in your life is more important than that particular golf shot," said Kite. "We all have families and jobs, and there are more important things than one shot, but for those few seconds, there's nothing more important than taking dead aim."

**Hit a club that gives you the best chance to keep the ball in the fairway. Here, I'm hitting a 3-wood to the corner of the dogleg, where the landing area is fairly wide.**

your shots around the green, so the additional practice will do more to lower your scores than hitting balls on the range will.

## 6. Make a Full Rehearsal Swing

As difficult as it is for most amateurs to take their range game to the first tee, they struggle even more to reproduce their rehearsal swing. They make a nice, tension-free practice swing, then they walk up to their ball and start chopping wood. Because there's an actual ball and target (and, in many cases, a perceived outcome) attached to the real shot, their swings are anything but loose and smooth.

To remedy this problem, I have my students practice a tension-free swing on the range and then transfer it over to the first tee. I have them make five or more practice swings and rate each, with 1 being the tightest and 5 being the freest swing (no tension) they can make. When they produce a 5 or close to it, they place a ball on a tee and see if they can match the same swing. You can do this on the first tee as well, limiting your practice swings, of course, to one or two swings.

I find that this drill gives amateurs a better awareness for the club and where their swing tends to get tight or too quick. Once you can pinpoint where these blindspots are, you can learn to slow down through these areas. This will help you replicate your practice swing more often on the first tee.

Another good range drill is to tee up five balls in succession and, with either a mid-iron or a wood, work down the line and hit each ball without stopping. You'll discover that because you have so little time to think between swings, you start to strike the ball more solidly in the center of the clubface. If you can take this mentality to the first tee, and worry about nothing else but swinging the club, you should be very successful.

## 7. Go on the Defensive

On the first tee, the whole object is to keep the ball in play. To that end, you need to choose a club that affords you the best opportunity to place the ball in the fairway. In many instances, it's not a driver.

Take the first tee shot at Pebble Beach, for example. It's not very long (from the tips, the par-4 plays 380 yards), but the longer you carry the ball off the tee, the narrower the fairway becomes. It's almost like hitting to a fairway the shape of a wine bottle, and the farther you drive it into the neck of the bottle, the more the fairway slopes from left to right. It's very common to see tee shots run off into the trees on the right-hand side of the fairway, leaving no approach into the green.

However, if you lay up too far back, you've got a long iron into a very small green, which is extremely difficult to hold. Ideally, you want a club you can hit about 220 yards off the tee, leaving an approach shot in the neighborhood of 160–170 yards. From there, you should be able to get down in three shots and make your par. If you carry your driver approximately 220 yards, then go with your driver, but if it's a 3-wood or hybrid distance for you, take the more defensive approach and hit that club— whatever will put you in the fairway.

The tee shot on the par-5 18th hole at Pebble Beach is one of the most intimidating and breathtaking in golf.

# Chapter 2

# Driving with Confidence

**C**ompared to the other clubs in your bag, the driver is the only one that doesn't have a maximum distance to it. A good player can hit his 7-iron 160–165 yards, but he's not stretching it much farther. If he has to, he'll reach for the next-longest club in his bag. But with the driver, there is no longer or more powerful club in the bag.

That's why golfers—and manufacturers—are always trying to figure out ways to get more distance out of the driver, whether it be through better technique, a longer club shaft, a higher COR (Coefficient of Restitution, or spring-like effect), or more clubhead speed. Think about it: When was the last time you were satisfied with the distance you hit one of your drives? If you blasted one 240 yards, you wanted to hit your next one 260, then 270, and so on.

Because the driver has no top end to it, golfers are always swinging for the fences. This can lead to all sorts of trouble because while the driver may be the longest club in your bag, it's also the hardest to control. It has the least amount of loft of any club in your bag—with the exception of the putter—which makes it very unforgiving. You might hit it 250 yards, but what good is that if it's 40 yards off-line?

When a student of mine tells me they're in the market for a new driver, I will quiz them about their current driver. "Do you keep the ball in play with it?" "Can you shape the ball consistently in the direction you want?" "Are you good with it under pressure?" If their answer to most of these questions is yes, I encourage them to stick with what they have. In most

# Laird's Lessons

**PEBBLE BEACH**
*GOLF ACADEMY*

## Driving with Confidence

**1. Take a 15-Yard Penalty:** This simple exercise teaches you why a shorter tee shot stopping in the fairway beats a long shot into the rough every time.

**2. 3-Wood vs. Driver:** Learn why the 3-wood is a superior choice off the tee for many players, resulting in higher shots with less sidespin—thus more predictable drives.

**3. Select the Right Tee for *You*:** Many golfers play from a tee box too far back for their skill level. This exercise helps you pick the perfect one.

**4. Swing to a Conservative Target:** Your goal should not always be to hit the ball as far as possible. Learn how to play smart off every tee, striving to keep the ball in play.

**5. Learn to Be a Player, Not a Golfer:** Golfers stand in the tee box and hope they don't slice it this time. Players accept that they usually slice their drives and plan for the likely outcome.

**6. Choosing a Target:** Dead straight is rarely the best line for a tee shot. Learn to match your target to both your swing and the layout of the hole.

**7. Swing All Clubs the Same Tempo:** Drills employed by Vijay Singh and Tom Watson will help you master this all-important concept for improving your game.

cases, people purchase a new driver because they want more distance, not because their old driver is underperforming. And when they do this, it's not uncommon to see them searching for a new driver about a year later.

First and foremost, find a driver that you're friends with, meaning one that is easy to hit and control. A friendly driver is a predictable driver; it keeps you in play even when you fail to make your best swing. It's like your best girl or your favorite dog. Resist the temptation to buy a new driver that promises 20 more yards and stay with what works for you. It might not be the driver you hit the farthest; it might be the one you hit consistently with the same shape and trajectory. If you can find a driver that's easy to hit and is long, then you truly have a magic club.

## 1. Take a 15-Yard Penalty

The next time you're playing alone or there are very few golfers on the course, try the following exercise. Hit driver off the tee as you normally would, except any time you miss the fairway and can't advance your next shot onto the green, march the ball out laterally to the fairway and take a 15-yard penalty against yourself. Step off 15 yards backward, as if your favorite NFL team was being penalized for a personal foul, and then play your next shot from there. Continue to do this every time you find yourself in trouble off the tee. March off a 15-yard penalty, drop the ball, and hit your next shot from the fairway.

Perform this exercise a few times, and you'll quickly discover why length is secondary to being in the short grass. You'll lower your handicap because you're playing from the fairway, not from a position where you have to

To see how important it is to keep the ball in the fairway, try this little game: 1) Retrieve your errant tee shot; 2) Walk the ball laterally into the fairway; 3) March off a 15-yard penalty (backward) against yourself; 4) Drop the ball and play your next shot from there. You'll find it much easier to score from the fairway, even if your ball is farther back.

① ② ③ ④

rescue yourself and get the ball back into play. Keep this in mind when you're thinking of buying a new driver. It's more important to find a driver you can keep in play than one you can wallop 30 yards farther but can't control.

## 2. 3-Wood vs. Driver

If you can't find a driver you can perform consistently with, then consider hitting a 3-wood off the tee. The average golfer hits a 3-wood farther than he does a mishit driver and in many cases farther than a well-struck driver. That's because with the additional loft, players have an easier time launching the ball up in the air with a 15-degree 3-wood. The ball travels higher, with less sidespin, and therefore flies straighter. By launching the ball higher in the air, gravity has less chance to overtake it, thus generating more carry.

Players who lack the clubhead speed necessary to launch the ball up in the air with only eight or nine degrees of loft need the extra loft of a 3-wood. That is the only way they're going to generate the kind of backspin and height they need to carry the ball a reasonable distance off the tee. They might lose some yardage, but the probability of hitting the ball higher and in play is much greater. The other advantage to hitting a 3-wood is that it looks friendlier to hit than a driver. It doesn't have such a big head, therefore there's less temptation to try to help the ball up in the air.

On many holes, such as the short par-4s or those where you need to keep the ball short of trouble, the 3-wood is the best choice off the tee. If you're playing a 350-yard hole, a 200-yard drive is going to put you at the 150-yard marker, a very reasonable, safe distance from which to approach the green. Most players can certainly hit their 3-wood 200 yards, so why risk smashing driver and missing the fairway when there's little to be gained from an extra 20–25 yards?

Good players get excited when they have the ability to predict the outcome before the event. Using the example above, they know that if they hit their 3-wood, they're going to have 100 or so yards into the green for their next shot. That allows them to swing away with confidence off the tee. Driving is all about confidence and finding a club that you can hit in play consistently. The 3-wood is the definition of a confidence club.

## 3. Select the Right Tee for *You*

There are five sets of tees at Pebble Beach Golf Links, ranging from 5,249 yards (red) to 7,040 yards (black). Determining which set of tees is best suited for your skill level, and playing from these tees, is the first step in becoming a successful driver of the golf ball.

Most golfers play a course that's way too long for them. Either they're afraid to speak up because their playing partners are using a different set of tees—and for speed of play purposes, they don't want to change tees—or their ego gets in the way of common sense. In most cases, it's the latter. I like to use the analogy of a basketball shooter when it comes to choosing from which tees to play. Most guys would rather go to the three-point line to attempt a shot than drive in for a lay-up because there's more gratification to making the three-pointer.

Play the right set of tees for your skill level and length. Here, I'm teeing it up from the gold tees (487 yards) on the par-5 6th hole. If the average length of your second shot (on par-4s) is more than a 5-iron distance, you're playing tees that are too long for you.

It's a longer shot, and it's worth more points; never mind that the odds of making the shot from long range are much less than from right underneath the basket. The problem with this approach in golf is that by picking the longer shot, you're only making it more difficult on yourself to keep the ball in play. And while you think you might be helping speed of play by playing from the middle or back tees, in reality you'll waste more time because you'll always be hitting out of trouble.

Here is a simple formula to help you determine which set of tees is right for you: first, take the average distance you hit your 5-iron (for the purpose of this exercise, let's say it's 160 yards), then multiply it by 36. That gives you 5,760 yards, which is the approximate yardage you should be playing from, plus or minus 150 yards. (The closest set of tees to this number at Pebble Beach would be the white tees, at 6,116 yards.) If you hit your 5-iron 160 yards, and you're playing from a set of tees that's 6,400 yards or longer, you're not going to be hitting 5-irons in for your second shots. Play a set of tees that will reward you with a 5-iron approach (or less) if you hit a good drive on a par-4. You'll spend more time actually playing the game, instead of constantly hitting a 3-wood into the green or laying up, and you'll shoot lower scores.

## 4. Swing to a Conservative Target

If I were to ask the first 10 golfers teeing off No. 1 at Pebble Beach one morning if they planned to be offensive (i.e., aggressive) or defensive with their opening tee shot, eight would say offensive. They'd tell me their goal would be to cut the corner of the dogleg, leaving a short-iron approach into the green. Almost all amateurs think that way. They believe that the goal of every tee shot is to hit the ball as far as possible, so they go for the big drive because *maybe* they'll be left with a short iron into the green. But what happens if they slice their tee shot into the trees on No. 1, or they hit through the dogleg into the first or second fairway bunker on the left? Now they're in full scramble mode for the remainder of the hole and will be lucky to make par.

The two trees in the middle of the 18th fairway create a good target off the tee, safely away from the ocean on the left.

The best players in the world are always defensive off the tee, because they know the most important thing is to keep the ball in play. Sure, they'll take a mighty big rip on occasion, but they're doing so to a conservative target. A perfect example of what I mean by playing strong to conservative targets came during the 1994 AT&T Pebble Beach National Pro-Am. The semiretired Johnny Miller, making a rare PGA TOUR appearance, nursed a one-shot lead over Tom Watson heading into the 72nd hole of regulation. Realizing that the one mistake he couldn't make on No. 18 was to hit the ball left, Miller eliminated any chance he had of finding the ocean by moving the ball back in his stance and playing a low Chi Chi Rodriguez push-draw into the center of the fairway. The ball didn't travel very far, about 220 yards, but it served its purpose: it kept him in play. He then chased a 2-iron up the fairway, wedged on, and two-putted for the victory.

"It was a well-played hole but ugly, if you want to call it that," said Miller. "They were low, little draws I hit on purpose. They eliminated the problem. [Lee] Trevino told me if you're nervous or choking just hit it low; it doesn't have time to get off-line. So I learned a lot by watching him under pressure, and Chi Chi."

Another prime example of this defensive mentality came at the 2000 U.S. Open at Pebble Beach. Tiger Woods, leading by an astonishing 15 shots, came to the 543-yard 18th with a chance to establish a new U.S. Open scoring record with a birdie. The hole was playing downwind, and the fairway was drying up, so reaching the green in two was well within his capacity. But what did Tiger do? He hit 4-iron off the tee! Then he laid up to about 120 yards, wedged on, two-putted, and walked off with a record-tying score of 272 (12-under par). Tiger could've hit a bunch of balls into the ocean and still won the tournament easily, but he took a conservative approach and played the hole the way it was designed to be played. "I wanted to have a day where I made no bogeys," Woods said afterward. "That was my goal from the beginning of the day: no bogeys." When Woods won the 2006 British Open at Hoylake, he did so hitting driver just once in 72 holes, stinging the fairways with his 2-iron and 3-wood. Great champions take the club that's best suited to put the ball in play off the tee. That's playing the game.

Now, I'm not suggesting you should never hit driver. To the contrary: golf is meant to be fun, and what's more enjoyable than smoking a drive out there 250 or more yards? But when you do have the driver in your hands, remember that the first priority is to put the ball in play. To help you accomplish this, keep these keys in mind: 1) grip down on the club if you're worried about the ball reaching a fairway bunker or some other hazard, 2) play to the widest part of the fairway, always making sure to hit away from trouble, 3) understand what your shot tendencies are and where you want the ball to finish, 4) maintain a constant grip pressure so you can feel the weight of the club as it's swinging, and 5) focus on the tempo of your transition from your backswing to downswing, which should be smooth.

If your tendency is to fade or slice your drives, tee the ball up on the far right-hand side of the tee box and aim down the left side of the fairway, as I'm doing here.

## 5. Learn to Be a Player, Not a Golfer

When you're hitting to a fairway where water or out of bounds is predominantly in play, and you have to eliminate one side of the fairway, it's important you make an honest assessment of who you are: Are you a golfer or a player? If you are a player, you understand that your tendency is to fade the ball off the tee. If you hit 10 shots, eight of them are going to curve somewhat to the right. Using the par-4 10th hole at Pebble Beach as an example, you'd want to tee the ball up on the far right-hand side of the tee box—as close to the marker and ocean as possible—aim down the left side of the fairway, and play your

normal ball flight. You'll also know how far it is to the cluster of fairway bunkers on the left side of the fairway, in case you hit the ball straight.

If you're a golfer, then you stand on the tee and hope this is the one time you don't slice your drive. You stick your peg in the middle of the tee box, aim down the center of the fairway, and make your normal swing. Then, when the ball bounces off the cliffs into the ocean or onto the beach below, you act surprised instead of knowing that your tendency is to slice.

Don't be a golfer. We all have certain tendencies, and we need to use them to our advantage. What do all golfers want? They want more consistency. Well, if you know your ball is going to fade to the right eight times out of 10, then why not aim down the left side of the fairway and play for the fade? If you're able to repeat the same shot shape and trajectory on most of your drives, then you have a consistent pattern and predictable outcome to help guide you to hitting more fairways.

## 6. Choosing a Target

Time after time, the average golfer stands on the tee and tries to hit his drive dead straight. Not even the best players in the world try to hit the ball perfectly straight because they're

**The 8th hole at Pebble Beach plays to a blind fairway. On the tee, my starting line is the right side of the house and my finish line the dome-shaped window. If I were a fader of the ball, I'd start my drive at the left side of the house and curve it back toward the window.**

**Tempo is the rate of speed at which your hands, arms, torso, and club move together. It's how these parts move in relationship to one another.**

trying to curve it. If they hit it straight it's usually by accident. When you contact the ball, you're going to impart some degree of backspin (which creates lift) and sidespin (which creates curvature) to the ball. The latter is extremely important when it comes to choosing a target off the tee because it's most responsible for where your ball winds up. Most amateurs don't realize this or, as I mentioned above, don't plan for it. They have a starting line in mind when they take aim at the fairway but no finish line. That's why so often the ball starts online, or just where the player aimed, and much to their dismay finishes 30 or 40 yards off that line.

When you choose your target, make sure you pick out a starting line and a finishing line, factoring in how much you want your ball to curve—or, how far it generally curves. Let's take the par-4 8th hole at Pebble Beach as an example. The tee shot plays to a blind fairway so it's very important you have a good target to

zone in on. In this case, it's the dome-shaped window on the late Leonard Firestone's house up on the hills overlooking Pebble Beach. It's directly in your line of sight, and if you can hit your tee shot in line with the windows, you'll have a manageable shot over the deep oceanic chasm to the green below. The window is your finish line, so if you want the ball to end up relatively close to the desired landing area, and you're a fader of the ball, then you've got to start your ball at the left side of the house to end up at the window. Conversely, if you like to draw the ball, you'll need to start the ball at the right side of the house. If you want no business hitting over the cliff, then you'll want your tee shot to finish well left of the house. It's no different than a putt that has a lot of break to it: if the ball breaks sharply from left to right, then your start line has to be a couple of balls left of the hole, on the high side, if you want the ball to hit the cup.

## 7. Swing All Clubs the Same Tempo

I was a last-second fill-in for an ill Frank Nobilo at the 2004 AT&T Pebble Beach National Pro-Am and was fortunate enough to play alongside Vijay Singh for the second and third rounds. Vijay was at the top of his game then (he would win nine PGA Tour events in '04 and even snatch the world's No. 1 ranking away from Tiger Woods) and striking the ball better than ever. After a few holes, he recognized that I could play the game a little bit, and we got to talking. I remember asking him what it is he worked on, and he said two things—grip pressure and tempo.

One way to regain your tempo on the course is to take some practice swings starting from a three-quarter position (in the follow-through). This will encourage your body and club to stay together and improve your sequencing of motion.

# Your Driver as Teacher

One interesting note about the driver: because it has so little loft, it tends to magnify what you're doing wrong in your full swing. In fact, it's the best club in the bag to identify swing faults and correct them. If, for example, you tend to slice or pop up your driver, then you can expect to take a deep divot with your short irons and hit the ball a little heavy at times. If you tend to sky your driver, then your backswing is too vertical, or up and down, which causes you to chop down on the ball. The easiest way to fix this is to lower your right shoulder and get behind the ball more at address, which will promote a wider, flatter backswing and a shallower angle of approach into the ball.

I often have my students warm up with the driver first on the range, instead of the traditionally accepted wedges. I have them take full swings with low energy, which lets them know if they have a path or face issue with their swing. If they do, they have plenty of time to correct it on the range before they hit the first tee. Swinging the longest and lightest club in their bag first also helps them gain a good feel for the proper tempo in their swing. The ball is also on the tee, which gives you a boost of confidence, and you start out making the most complete swing you can to establish a good sense of rhythm, balance, and timing.

Tempo is the rate of speed at which your hands, arms, torso, and club move together. It's how these parts move in relationship to one another. Most amateurs try to overpower the ball with their arms and shoulders because they associate the driver with distance. What they don't realize is that the driver, while being the longest club in the bag, is also the lightest. It doesn't have to be swung that hard to hit the ball far. The key is to keep your club and body moving together so you do hit the sweet spot on the club, because any mishit with a driver is going to be magnified due to its lack of loft.

When I asked Vijay how he worked on tempo, he said he used a numeric metronome of sorts using the number *17*, or *seven-teen*. About two feet into his backswing, he would internally start to say the word *seeeeven-teen* to himself, so by the time the clubhead reached impact he would be at *teen*. This would allow him to keep the same tempo for the entire round.

It should be noted that Vijay, and all good players, swing each club in their bag at the same tempo, from sand wedge to driver. The driver has to travel the greatest distance and therefore produces the most clubhead speed. But that speed needs to be developed gradually; it shouldn't be forced, otherwise you'll use up your power prematurely before the clubhead arrives at the ball.

If you feel like your tempo is getting quick during the course of a round, and you need to rediscover it, try the drill from Tom Watson in Chapter 1, holding your driver upside down so you're gripping it by the neck with both hands, just above the clubhead. Make five or six

swings, each time getting the handle to make a swoosh sound through impact. Turn the club around again so you're gripping it normally and take a few more practice swings. You should have a better feel for the weight of the clubhead, which will help you swing it in rhythm with your body. Watson used this drill often in winning his five British Open championships. His hands would get so cold that he'd lose all sensitivity for the club, and this drill would help him get that feel back.

Another thing you can do is take a few practice swings off to the side, starting your swing from a three-quarter-length position in the follow-through. From here, swing your arms back all the way to the top of your backswing and then down again into a full finish. What this drill does is help you shift your weight onto your front foot as you start the club down from the top, so your lower body remains in sync with the club. It's a great way to regain your tempo because it puts the correct sequence of motion back together; your feet should always lead your hands on the downswing.

You can also make some baseball swings at approximately knee height. This will encourage the club to swing more around your body on an inside-to-inside path, which helps you to hit a draw. The more vertical the club swings, the more likely the ball will fade or slice.

With the beach looming to the right, there's little margin for error on approach shots to the par-4 9th and 10th holes at Pebble Beach.

# Approach Shots

Once your tee shot finds the fairway, your work is far from over. Your next shot, whether it be a lay-up or an approach into the green, can mean the difference between a good score and disaster. Yet so many golfers relax on their second shot—they don't put as much preparation or focus into it as they do their tee ball—and thus pay a steep penalty when they misfire and leave themselves with an impossible up and down. There is nothing more frustrating than carding bogey or worse after hitting a perfect drive, especially when you know it could have been avoided.

For this chapter, we will focus on the approach shot, with tips and strategies to help you hit more greens in regulation. This way, you can take full advantage of being in the fairway.

## 1. Rehearse a Preshot Checklist

When I watch golfers hit balls on the driving range, they almost never practice their preshot routine—if they have one at all. They hit shot after shot without changing targets, checking their alignment, or taking a moment to visualize the type of shot they want to play. They're in rapid-fire mode. If you watch the Tour pros, they'll take time between shots. They'll observe what the ball is doing in the air and process this information before they start their routine for the next shot. They may even take time to chat with their caddie or another pro. On average, they go 30 seconds to a minute between shots, whereas the average golfer takes about 10 seconds. On the course, you're going to have a

# Laird's Lessons

PEBBLE BEACH
GOLF ACADEMY™

## Approach Shots

**1. Rehearse a Preshot Checklist:** There are five questions that golfers should ask themselves before every approach shot. This exercise is part of a preshot routine that every golfer should develop, practice on the range, and transfer to the course.

**2. Turn Your Don'ts into Dos:** Learn to replace the negative thoughts floating through your head (about avoiding the worst possible outcomes) with positive commands focused on achieving your goals for the shot.

**3. Know Where to Miss:** Good players are aware of the trouble areas and traps built into the holes by the architect and can identify safe places for less-than-perfect shots to land.

**4. Play to the Entire Green:** Forget about shooting for the flagstick—the green is a much larger target and one that is easier to hit than a 10-foot circle around the hole.

**5. Take One More Club:** Most golfers overestimate their average distance with a given club. Moving up one club will allow a smoother swing and result in more greens hit.

**6. Forced Carries: Focus on Execution:** Learn how to approach any carry over an intimidating hazard with "second-ball" mentality and forget about all the negative consequences of the shot.

few minutes before you play your next ball, so it makes sense to build in time between shots on the practice range.

Because he hasn't practiced a preshot routine, the average golfer has no cadence—or series of checks—to help him process all of the information he needs to execute the shot properly. That's why you see so many golfers tense up over the ball: either they're unsure if they have the right club in their hands, or they're running through various outcomes, usually negative, in their head. They have no idea what shot they want to play, and many times they'll hit the one they're most trying to avoid.

The preshot routine is one aspect of the game that is easily transferable from the range to the course, if you practice it. Here are five questions you want to ask yourself when preparing to hit a shot. The more you familiarize yourself with this checklist, the easier time you'll have processing all of the information on the course, so you can make the clearest decision and the right one for the shot at hand.

**1) What is my lie?** Is the ball sitting up in the rough or well down in the grass? Is there nothing but hard ground under the ball? The lie is going to dictate what you can and cannot do with the golf ball. For example, if it's sitting down and the grass is growing against you, you're going to have no choice but to pitch the ball back in play.

**2) What is the slope of the fairway?** Is it uphill or downhill? Is the ball above or below my feet? The ball is going to have a tendency to curve in the direction of the slope. For example, the fairway on the par-4 10th hole at Pebble Beach slopes from left to right, toward

The fairway on the par-4 10th hole slopes significantly from left to right; approach shots to this green tend to curve in the same direction.

the ocean, so the ball will tend to move in that direction. Uphill, the ball has a tendency to fly higher and curve to the left; downhill, it does the opposite, so you want to hit a more-lofted club and aim farther to the left to compensate for the ball moving to the right.

**3) What is the wind doing?** Pay special attention to the treetops and which direction they're blowing because wind has a greater effect on the ball at its altitude up in the air than at ground level.

**4) What type of shot do I want to play?** This goes back to chapter 2 and choosing both a starting point and an ending point for each shot. Using No. 10 as an example once again, because the ball is below your feet, it's going to want to curve from left to right. Therefore, the best play is to start the ball at the left greenside bunker and allow the slope to fade it toward the center of the

**For this shot to find the putting surface, I'm going to have to start my ball at the left greenside bunker (inset) and allow the slope to fade it toward the middle of the green.**

smallish green. If you aim directly at the flag, chances are it's going to wind up in the ocean. Golfers never see that coming.

**5) How is the ball going to react on the green?** If the greens are firm, then you'll need to play to a shorter distance, allowing the ball to release and roll; if they're soft, you'll need to carry the ball farther onto the putting surface, almost to the flag, because the ball is not going to roll very much. You also have to consider the slope of the green. Most greens are sloped from back to front, sometimes severely, so it's often best to hit your approach shot short, leaving it below the flagstick so you have an uphill putt.

Before each approach shot, take a timeout to run through this checklist. With a little practice, it will not only become faster and easier, but it will take away a lot of the guesswork that can doom your approach shots.

## 2. Turn Your Don'ts into Dos

Staring at your approach shot on the par-4 9th hole at Pebble Beach, it's hard not to notice the beach to the right of the green or the deep bunker short and left of the green. The course architect put these hazards there for a reason—he's trying to distract you from executing the shot at hand—and considering how most golfers will do anything possible to avoid these hazards, he generally succeeds.

Most recreational golfers associate hazards with penalties or the inability to hit certain types of shots: "I don't want to miss right because I'll be in the ocean," or "I don't want to go in the bunker because I'll never get out." They give themselves all types of negative commands

that interfere with their ability to think clearly and positively. It's like opening up 15 programs on your computer all at once; if you don't close any, it's no wonder the computer crashes.

It's the same thing with all of these negative thought processes going on in your head. You can't focus your attention on the middle of the green when all you're thinking about is what happens if you slice it or come up short in the bunker. When our bodies are stressed, it also makes it difficult to execute a tension-free swing to hit that shot.

The word *don't* is a four-letter word to golfers. What you have to do is replace it with a two-letter word—*do*. How often do you go shopping and say to yourself, "I don't want to buy that cereal," or "I don't need any more ice cream?" Probably never. You go there with an intention of buying something. You know which aisle the cereal is in and what kind of meat you want for Saturday's cookout, and you go get it. Take the same approach to golf and replace any negative commands you have with positive ones: "*Do* start the ball at the left edge of the bunker and fade it back to the center of the green." "*Do* carry your ball to the front-center portion of the green, two-putt, and walk away with par." If you find yourself thinking about the worst-case scenario, talk yourself through it and turn it around into a positive: "If I hit into the bunker, that's okay because with my sand game I can get it up and down easily."

Another thing you can do to stop obsessing about the outcome is divert your attention elsewhere, like to the top of the flagstick or a cluster of trees off in the hillside behind the green. With my junior golfers, I use the image of picking off a burglar in the distance. I have them imagine that there's a thief standing on the roof of their neighbor's house—maybe it's home to the Three Bears—and he's going to sneak down through the second-floor window and rob their home. I ask them, "Can you, with your golf ball, knock off the burglar?" Now their mind's attention is transfixed on that burglar and creating the right amount of trajectory and curvature they need on their shot to pick him off. It moves their attention to the target, so they can hit different shots.

It's the same mind-set you might have on the driving range when the ball picker comes into your line of play: what do you want to do? Of course you want to hit the vehicle. The average golfer could use that kind of playful attitude about the game so that his mind doesn't get fixated on the ocean or some other penalizing hazard.

## Johnny Miller: Knock Down the Pin

During his professional playing career, there was no better iron player than Johnny Miller. He had tremendous control of his distances; in fact, during one of his wins at Pebble Beach (Miller was the only player to capture the Bing Crosby/AT&T Pebble Beach National Pro-Am in three different decades: 1974, '87, and '94), Miller recalls hitting 59 consecutive greens in regulation. "I finally hit the lip of the bunker on No. 5 in the fourth round," Miller said of the course's first par-3. "Another foot, and it would've been stiff."

Miller's key to hitting so many greens?

"My most important thought was this, 'Would you guys hurry up and hit because I can't wait to hit it; this is going to be fun,'" said Miller, who won the '94 AT&T at age 46 despite playing just five PGA TOUR events over the three previous seasons. "That was my thought process every time. I can't wait to hit this shot and knock the pin right out of the green."

Miller says amateurs today lose sight of the fun aspects of the game and dwell too much on the negatives in their preshot routine. He recommends taking a more positive, assertive approach.

"The biggest problem people have is that as we get older we learn the word 'consequences,' and that's what ruins all of our dreams and outstanding moments," said Miller. "We think, *Gee, if I hit it here this could happen*. Kids don't do that. When you're young you just see the pin and go for it. You don't think about what could happen, because then you can't even produce a golf swing. The big thing is I played real quickly, like [Tom] Watson did. I would pick the shot and just hit the dang thing. I wouldn't over-think it. I tried to be positive and say 'this is going to be fun.'"

## 3. Know Where to Miss

Good players always have a bailout spot in the back of their mind, a place they can go if they're unsure of the shot they want to hit or if the risk of going at the flag is too great. I remember hosting a clinic with David Duval shortly after he shot a 59 in the final round of the 1999 Bob Hope Chrysler Classic. Duval was discussing approach shots and told the crowd that any time he was unsure of a shot, he would play a club or two less and hit the ball to the front of the green or short of the green. From there, he'd have an uphill chip or a putt and a decent shot at getting the ball up and down for par. On the flip side, if he played a shot he wasn't entirely committed to and missed badly, he could find himself short-sided or worse and facing a sure bogey. By choosing to play more conservatively and hit to a safe zone, he took the potential for a big number out of the equation.

In preparation for the 1999 U.S. Open at Pinehurst No. 2, noted golf instructor Chuck Cook got his hands on a yardage book and, using a red Sharpie, marked it up like he was grading a fourth-grade essay. He and Payne Stewart walked each and every hole, with Cook placing red Xs in those trouble areas off the tee and on or around the greens that he thought Stewart should play away from. Stewart was resistant at first, but he followed Cook's strategy and went on to win the U.S. Open.

The lesson here is to play the hole as it's designed—i.e., play smart. Most amateurs fire away at the flag without giving any thought whatsoever as to why the architect placed a bunker here or a pond there. Make sure you've

> **If every time you missed the green you left the ball in a spot where you still had an opportunity to get up and down, you'd eliminate the big number and keep your scores low.**

got enough club to clear any hazard that may be fronting the green, and in cases where the trouble is to one side of the green, hit away from it. Look around the hole to see if there's anywhere you can bail out short, long, left, or right of the green and still have a reasonable chance at saving par.

In her book, *Golf Annika's Way*, Hall of Famer Annika Sorenstam wrote: "Golf is not just a game of great shots. It's a game of bad shots, too. The champions are the ones who hit the fewest bad shots—and who are smart enough to keep their bad shots from being terrible." This is great advice. If every time you missed the green you left the ball in a spot where you still had an opportunity to get up and down, you'd eliminate the big number and keep your scores low. You're going to miss many greens in your lifetime, but how well you manage those misses is very important.

# 4. Play to the Entire Green

When Manuel de la Torre, the longtime head golf professional at Milwaukee Country Club, was interviewed for the position more than 50 years ago, one of the questions he was asked was how he'd go about improving every member's handicap. De la Torre, a member of the World Golf Teachers Hall of Fame, said he could lower the entire club's handicap by two strokes instantly. Of course, everybody wanted to know how, so he was called back for a second interview. When quizzed about it, de la Torre said he'd let them in on his secret only if he was hired for the job.

Naturally, they hired him, and de la Torre's answer to the question was to remove the flagstick from each hole. It was as simple as that. His reasoning was that if you pulled the flagstick from all 18 holes, you would stop thinking about hitting the perfect shot into

On most approach shots, such as this one into the 9th green at Pebble Beach (1), you're better off removing the flagstick from your thought process (2) and aiming the for entire green (3). The larger your target, the more room you have to fit the ball and the easier it is to make a relaxed, free swing.

every green—tight to the flagstick—and focus on hitting the ball anywhere on the green. Instead of playing to a small, defined target (the flagstick), you would play to a much larger one (the entire green), which would free you up to make a more confident, easy swing and, consequently, hit more greens.

This is a great way to look at your approach shots. Now, obviously, you can't ask the course superintendent to remove the flagstick from every green, but you can visualize each hole without one. Try it the next time you're playing: remove the flagstick from your thought process and visualize your target as one big green. Imagine how many balls you could fit side to side on the putting surface; we're talking hundreds. You'll be surprised how much easier it is to hit the green when your target isn't so precise and your margin for error is much greater.

For the average golfer, any approach shot that lands on the green is a good result because you're then giving yourself an opportunity to putt on your next shot. This is especially true on longer approach shots of 150 yards or more: play to the middle of the green. If you hit more greens in regulation during your round, you only stand to have more scoring opportunities. Hit all 18 greens in regulation, and I can guarantee you that you'll drop more than the two strokes de la Torre had promised the members in Milwaukee.

## 5. Take One More Club

If I were to ask the average golfer how far he hits his 7-iron, he might tell me 150 or 155 yards. He'd give me the distance for that 1-in-10 perfectly struck golf shot, not the average of the other nine 7-irons he hit. Most golfers do that; they're under the impression that they hit the ball farther than they actually do. It's very much an ego thing: just as we always tend to think we're thinner or taller than we actually are, we think we hit the ball farther in the air than we actually do.

The reality is that most golfers only have a vague idea how far they hit their 7-iron or any club in their bag, for that matter. They haven't any clue how far the ball is going to travel, but they have this large number in their head that represents their maximum carry distance. As a result, they swing hard and have all kinds of trouble maintaining good rhythm and balance. Almost inevitably, their approach shot comes

**When playing slightly uphill, it's always advisable to take one more club (i.e., an 8-iron versus a 9-iron), as I'm doing here on the par-4 4th hole.**

# Jack Nicklaus: Look for a Safety Net

When Jack Nicklaus redesigned the par-3 5th hole at Pebble Beach in the late 1990s, he replaced an uphill, inland hole and converted it into a relatively short, downhill par-3 with the green nestled along the coastline. Like most par-3s, he provided a small bailout area short and left of the green to give players a safety net and a chance to make their par should they not want to gamble and fire at the flag.

"I felt like with the ocean on the right, we needed a little bit of a fairway cushion on the left," said Nicklaus, who won the 1972 U.S. Open at Pebble Beach and three Bing Crosby National Pro-Ams. "That's why I gave the fairway bailout, because I felt the ocean was difficult enough. You had to have some leeway on the other side. You have to try to create a situation where the hole is fair."

Not all of the par-3s at Pebble Beach afford you the chance to bail out. The 7th hole, for example, is surrounded by bunkers, and the ocean looms behind the green and also to the right. It's a fairly short hole, but if you miss the green, you can find yourself in a heap of trouble. The 17th hole, site of Nicklaus' famous 1-iron at the '72 Open, does give you room to bail out to the right, but if the pin is tucked on the left side (as is normally the case in the U.S. Open) you're faced with a delicate pitch or chip across the figure-eight shaped green.

If you're confronted with a difficult par-3 hole, examine the area around the green closely and see if the architect gave you a safe place to bail out. If there is none, don't be afraid to lay up short of the trouble and play the hole like a short par-4.

"We are not robots, and human error is going to be a factor, so you have got to be able to compensate for that," said Nicklaus. "Take the 16th hole at Cypress Point Club. They placed a big fairway to the left, so the average golfer could play the hole as a par-4. If they had not done that, and left you with only one shot from tee to green, the most spectacular par-3 in the world would've been possibly the worst par-3 in the world. But because of the fairway, they've allowed many levels of golfers to play it. You have got to be able to give and take on a par-3 to make it work. There are some par-3s that don't have any give and take."

For more information on how to play par-3 holes, see Chapter 4.

up short of the green, where the architect has placed a bunker or some other hazard.

The next time you play, take one more club (i.e., a 6-iron versus a 7-iron) than you normally would for an approach shot of that distance and make a three-quarter swing. See how many greens you hit. You'll be able to swing smooth and easy, improving your balance and tempo. That will allow you to control your distances better and hit more greens.

The other advantage to playing one more club is that it leaves you with some insurance should your approach shot play slightly uphill. What most people don't realize is the uphill nature of shots: architects need to drain water from the green, so they build greens with some upward slope to them. That's why you see so many greens slope from back to front. An example of this is the par-4 1st hole at Pebble Beach. If you hit a decent tee shot, you're usually left with 120 to 125 yards to the flagstick. What people don't see is that the approach shot plays longer than the actual yardage (about half a club) because the green is slightly elevated to allow for drainage. It slopes from back to front and from left to right. If you play to the number on the yardage marker, you could very well find one of the two bunkers tightly guarding the green.

## 6. Forced Carries: Focus on Execution

The one approach shot at Pebble Beach that is most likely to get your heart pounding and your brain overthinking comes at the par-4 8th hole. No doubt if you've watched the AT&T over the years you've seen the giant oceanic chasm that separates the top portion of the fairway (or driving zone) from the green. At its widest point, it's only 120 yards to carry the ocean, but it seems so much farther than that.

Any time you have a forced carry of this magnitude, whether it's over water, deep fescue, gorse, or some other kind of imposing obstacle, it's essential that you shift your attention away from the trouble (i.e., the outcome). One of the ways to do that is to focus on making solid contact with the ball. Most amateurs mishit this shot and top it into the ocean because their swing bottoms out too early, behind the ball. Take one or two rehearsal swings before you step up to the shot and brush the turf where you would normally play your ball. Then get up to the ball and make the same exact swing while in the same rhythm, brushing the ground where the ball is. If you still wind up hitting the ball in the ocean, accept the result and move on; don't beat yourself up over it because the next time you find yourself in a similar spot, that bad result is more likely to stay with you.

Approach any forced carry with a "second-ball" mentality. Think about it: how many times have you hit a shot out of bounds or into a hazard and then stepped up to hit your next shot three feet from the hole? It happens all the time. You'll botch your first attempt, step up to the second one without even hesitating, and knock it stiff. Then you'll say, "Why couldn't I have done that the first time?" The reason why is because on your second attempt you weren't thinking about all of the consequences of the shot. You have to get in that mode where you're just thinking about executing the shot or brushing the grass; then you'll have more of a carefree attitude when you swing.

**Solid contact is essential if you are to carry a large hazard, such as the famous ocean chasm on the par-4 8th hole at Pebble Beach. Shift your focus away from the trouble and concentrate on brushing the ground where the ball is.**

Tour players approach every shot with a second-shot mentality. They have a preplay capability that they have practiced on the range and course that prepares them for tournament play. Jack Nicklaus would preplay the shot in his mind as if he were replaying it from a movie reel: he would see the trajectory, shape, and flight of the ball, and where it landed, before he ever took the club back. Tiger Woods does the same thing: he creates a picture with the intention of what he wants to do on a particular shot and then plays to the picture. The best players see the shot in their mind's eye so, as with a second-shot mentality, they have no fear of the outcome.

Even at 98 yards, the par-3 7th hole at Pebble Beach is one of the most imposing par-3s in all of golf.

# Chapter 4

# Playing the Par-3s

The four par-3s at Pebble Beach will inspire, deceive, and test every aspect of your game. Small, narrow greens, changing wind conditions, elevation swings, and stunning ocean vistas combine to make these holes a challenging par for any golfer.

Each par-3 is rich in history, too, starting with the 5th hole, which sits on a bluff some 50 feet above Stillwater Cove. Redesigned by Jack Nicklaus in 1998, this hole plays slightly downhill to a heavily bunkered green, radically different from its predecessor, which played as an uphill, inland, slightly doglegged par-3. It's longer (195 yards from the back tees) than the previous version but plays about the same length because of its downhill nature.

What makes this hole so tricky is that the green is disguised by several bunkers, every one of them built up to give off the illusion that the green is smaller than it is. But it's actually the second-largest green on the course. The back portion of the green is hollowed out and almost completely invisible off the tee because it's hidden by a large greenside bunker. During his record-breaking performance at the 2000 U.S. Open, this was the only par-3 that Tiger Woods bogeyed.

The 7th hole is one of the most photographed and dramatic par-3s in the world, not to mention one of the shortest. At 98 yards from the middle teeing ground, players will hit anything from a sand wedge to a midiron to the green below, depending on the wind conditions. Tom Kite, playing in the final group at the 1992 U.S. Open, hit a 6-iron from the tee; Kirk Triplett, teeing off in the morning's first group, hit a sand wedge. Even a putter isn't out of the question: at the 1950 Bing Crosby Pro-Am,

# Laird's Lessons

PEBBLE BEACH
GOLF ACADEMY™

## Playing the Par-3s

**1. Create a Perfect Lie:** Yes, you should tee the ball up, but exactly how high will vary depending on the size of the clubhead—and your individual swing.

**2. Grip Down when Between Clubs:** When there isn't a perfect club for the distance, select the longer club, choke down an inch or two, and take your normal swing.

**3. Avoid Sucker Pins:** Don't go hunting for a pin placed in a challenging spot. Instead, select a more conservative target, avoid trouble, and earn your par.

**4. Adjust Your Vision:** On par-3s with significant elevation changes, learn to compensate for the tendency for your eyes to drift left (on downhill holes) or right (on uphill holes).

the wind was blowing so strong that Sam Snead took out his flatstick and putted the ball down the hill into the front greenside bunker, from where he made par. It was the only par the hole yielded all day.

While one of the more overlooked holes at Pebble Beach, the par-3 12th can be a round-breaker because it takes a very precise shot to hit a wide but very narrow green. The left greenside bunker is almost as big as the green itself, and the presence of trees behind the green makes it difficult to gauge the wind.

Finally, there's the 17th hole, which at 208 yards from the black tees plays as the longest par-3 at Pebble Beach. In the first four U.S. Opens contested at Pebble Beach (1972, '82, '92, and 2000), this hole played the toughest in relation to par. The reason is because the hole plays downwind to a very narrow, hourglass-shaped green that is nearly impossible to hold coming in with a mid- or long iron. If you fire at the flagstick, chances are the ball will roll off the back of the green, leaving a downhill pitch from the rough that is extremely difficult to stop. Many players will purposely take a club less and hit their tee shot into the large greenside bunker fronting the green. There's a higher probability of making par from the bunker than from behind the green, which is exactly what Tiger Woods did in his final round of the 2000 U.S. Open.

Still, this hole has been the scene of some of the most dramatic moments in major-championship history. In what might have been his most memorable shot ever, Jack Nicklaus hit a 1-iron into this green at the 1972 U.S. Open that hit the flagstick and settled six inches from the hole. Nicklaus was on the wrong side of the 17th hole's magic at the 1982 U.S. Open, however, when Tom Watson pitched in from the rough for birdie in the final round to take a one-shot lead over Nicklaus. Watson's 2-iron approach was pin-high but released into the high, wiry rough—yet somehow he was able to hop in his short, delicate pitch.

There are typically four par-3 holes on every course, and each one presents a good scoring opportunity because the distance is already established, and you can tee the ball up. The difficult part is that you have only one shot to hit the green and two putts to make your par, and you know the course architect isn't going to make it easy for you. The following chapter will offer you some strategies and tips on how to play these par-3s, so you take the fewest number of strokes on these holes and walk away with some 2s and 3s on your scorecard.

## 1. Create a Perfect Lie

Ben Hogan was once asked if he teed the ball up on par-3s and said, "Son, I play for money." He teed the ball up because it gave him the best chance to make solid contact and knock the ball stiff.

In the old days, you might see a player kick up a tuft of grass and place the ball on top of the grass, but with modern equipment today, it makes a lot more sense to tee the ball up above the ground. What that does is give you a perfect lie; it also allows you to position the ball in line with the sweet spot of the club, so you can hit the ball more solidly for better distance control.

How high should you tee it up? It depends on the size of the clubhead. With today's perimeter-weighted game-improvement irons, the sweet spot is generally higher on the clubface—about four grooves up—so you want to tee the ball up about a half inch above the ground. Tee it up too low, and you're liable to catch the ball thin because there's so much mass to the sole of these clubs; conversely, if you tee it up too high, you're likely to contact the ball near the top of the clubface and not hit it very far. Make a swing that brushes the turf or knocks the tee out

The one advantage to par-3s is that you're allowed to tee the ball up to a perfect lie. Tee it up a half inch off the ground, which encourages you to contact the ball high on the clubface, near the sweet spot.

from under the ball, and you're going to catch the sweet spot of the club more often than not and have a greater chance of hitting the ball the right distance. If you're playing a thinner-blade iron or a club with a much smaller sole, then tee the ball lower because the sweet spot is likely to be farther down on the clubface. Experiment and see what works best for you.

## 2. Grip Down when Between Clubs

While each of the par-3s at Pebble Beach is unique in its own way, one thing they all share is a tendency to leave you in-between clubs. The targets are very small, which forces you to be very precise with your distances and requires some feel and imagination.

**When in-between clubs, take the longer of the two clubs and grip down an inch or two on the handle. With the longer club, you won't feel the urge to squeeze out a few more yards.**

# Arnold Palmer: Fire at the Middle of the Green

Pebble Beach has four very demanding par-3s. Some people may not group No. 7 in with the other three holes because it's so short (109 yards from the back tees), but as Arnold Palmer points out, it can take you out of a good round.

"It's a short hole, but it's a good hole," said Palmer, who never won at Pebble Beach but counts playing with the likes of Jack Lemmon, Phil Harris, and Gordon MacRae in the Crosby Pro-Am as his fondest memories of Pebble Beach. "It's a hole that requires a very exacting shot, and it's best to hit the ball at the middle of the green and go from there. Some players don't believe in that; they believe in going right at it [the flag]. If they're successful, that's fine, but if they're unsuccessful, the penalty is severe."

When Palmer designs a par-3 hole, he tries to distribute the trouble on all sides of the green. At the same time, he likes to give the player a break, or a means out, should he want to play the hole more conservatively.

"Of course, on some par-3s there is no way out," said Palmer. "The 17th at TPC Sawgrass, for example, is completely surrounded by water, and there are no alternatives. If you're looking for a conservative play, it's to hit to the middle of the green. In this case, hitting the ball in the middle of the green is very desirable because if you're successful at doing that, you're going to have a reasonable putt at birdie.

"The middle of the green on all of the par-3s [at Pebble Beach] is not a bad option."

The 7th hole, for example, plays only 98 yards downhill from the middle tees. It's not quite a full pitching wedge for most golfers, but it's too much distance to cover with a gap wedge. So what do you do? Most amateurs will take the longer of the two clubs (the PW) and swing easier, but that often forces a disconnection between the arms and the body and leads to a fat or thin shot. Most pros will take the shorter of the two clubs (the GW) and swing harder, leaving the ball below the flagstick. But what you also see many pros do is grip down on the longer of the two clubs and swing away. This shortens the lever and makes the club

perform less distance (about seven yards for every inch you grip down).

This is the method that I think makes most sense for the amateur golfer because it allows you to make your normal bread-and-butter swing without trying to squeeze a few more yards out of the club. It also eliminates the guesswork you get when you have to make a partial swing. You won't be making up a swing as you go along. If you're uncomfortable with, say, hitting a 4- or 5-iron into the green from 180 yards out (e.g., the tee shot on the par-3 12th at Pebble Beach), you're going to be much more successful choking down an inch or two on a hybrid club—which is more forgiving and easier to hit—and making your normal swing. You'll make a much smoother swing and contact the ball more toward the center of the clubface, hitting the ball the desired distance.

## 3. Avoid Sucker Pins

When Jack Nicklaus hit his infamous 1-iron to six inches on No. 17 at the 1972 U.S. Open, he wasn't taking dead aim at the flagstick. To the contrary: the wind was blowing hard over his right shoulder and knocking the ball down, and the only way he felt he could get the ball onto the putting surface was to aim at the right-hand portion of the hourglass-shaped green, away from the flag. Had he taken dead aim, Nicklaus would have probably been in the same area of thick rough where Tom Watson pitched in from 10 years later or, even worse, in the ocean. Nicklaus, however, pulled his tee shot left and received one of the kindest bounces of all time, as the ball jumped into the flagstick and dropped six inches from the hole.

The lesson here is that whenever the pin is tucked in the corner of the green or in a very narrow landing area—what is commonly known as a "sucker pin"—don't go straight at the flag

**When the pin is tucked to one side of the green, as it often is at Pebble's 17ᵗʰ hole (photos 1 and 2), it's best to ignore the flagstick and play to a more conservative target. On No. 17, the target is to the right of the front greenside bunker (photo 3), which leaves you with a long putt or fairly straight-forward pitch or chip across the green (photo 4).**

and put yourself in position to make bogey or worse. Play aggressively to a more conservative target, as we discussed in Chapter 2, and borrow some real estate away from the pin. The left pin placement on No. 17 is a big reason why that hole plays so tough in U.S. Opens: it's nearly impossible to stop a long iron there, unless you hit the stick like Nicklaus did. The wise decision is to aim 10 or 15 paces right of the pin and play to the fattest part of the green. Had he not done this, Nicklaus wouldn't have stumbled into such luck.

Another option you have on lengthy par-3s, such as the 17th, is to hit the ball to the front of the green or just short of the green and try to get up and down from there. Most architects will give you a way onto the green on longer par-3s, usually from in front of the green. On No. 17, the opening is to the right of the front greenside

bunker, a much shorter distance from the tee than the left pin location. From here, you can chip the ball across the green or use your putter.

The average dispersion rate—or distance the ball finishes away from the hole—on shots of 100 yards is about 20 feet on the PGA TOUR. For a 200-yard shot, it doubles to about 40 feet. What does this mean to the average golfer? It means that on most par-3s you should be very happy landing your tee shot anywhere on the green. Whether it's a short par-3 or a long one, it's always a good strategy not to hunt for the pin. The goal is to get the ball on the green and let your putter do the talking. Allow your putter to erase any mistakes you might make off the tee; you don't want to have to rely on your wedge to rescue you from the deep rough or some other impossible shortsided situation.

# Johnny Miller: Hit Your Go-To Shot

Johnny Miller knows a thing or two about making a hole in one. He's had 28 in his lifetime, around the same number as Jack Nicklaus. But as Miller likes to joke, "He made them all with the same shot. I made them with every kind of [ball] flight."

During his prime, Miller had grooved four different shots that he could call upon at any time, based on the amount of curve and trajectory that was required. He had the [Lee] Trevino fade for right pin locations, the [Tony] Lema high hook for front-left pin placements, a Chi Chi [Rodriguez] low hook for back-left pins, and his own ball, which traveled high and straight. Miller could hit it high or low, draw or fade it—whatever the situation demanded. That's what made him such a sniper on par-3s.

"I had so many shots developed that I had a few more green lights than most other players," said Miller. "I would see the pin and the hole location and say, 'Well, whose shot is this? Is it a Lema, a Trevino, a Chi Chi, or my own?' The bottom line is, if you have more shots, you have more chances to make a hole in one."

At the 1982 U.S. Open at Pebble Beach, which would become famous for Tom Watson's chip in from off the green on No. 17, Miller recorded one of three holes in one in the tournament. His came on the difficult par-3 12th hole, a 3-iron into a left-to-right wind with a back-left hole location he called "impossible." What's more remarkable is that several months later at the Pebble Beach Invitational, Miller made a hole in one on the exact same hole to the exact same pin location. Just as he did at the U.S. Open,

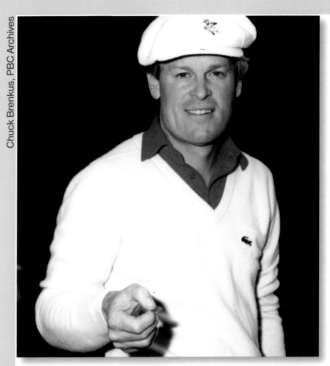

Chuck Brenkus, PBC Archives

he called on a Tony Lema high hook into the slice wind. The ball came down soft and trickled right into the hole. "It went in at the same miles per hour," said Miller. "People talk about visualization: I hit the identical shot, landed it in the identical spot, and rolled it in the exact same way."

Miller had the luxury of four shots he could turn to but suggests that most amateurs stick with their bread-and-butter shot on par-3s, whatever that may be. "You only have one shot, so play the percentage shot," said Miller. "If you have a wind or a hole location that fits your shot, then you should try to be reasonably aggressive with it, especially if it's a shorter distance. But otherwise, when you make three on any hole, you're not going to lose much ground. Just know that three is a great score, two is a bonus, and one is amazing."

On downhill par-3s like No. 7, it helps to aim at the right-hand portion of the green since the tendency is for the eyes to be pulled left.

## 4. Adjust Your Vision

A lot of par-3s will feature dramatic elevation changes, such as the 7th at Pebble Beach: the tee is perched some 40 feet above the green, which juts out into Carmel Bay. Because the hole plays so much downhill, there's a tendency for the eyes to drift left, because that's the direction they're being pulled as you look down. The greenside bunker to the left of the seventh green is the busiest bunker in the world for this very reason, because that's where everyone is mistakenly aiming.

As you set up to the ball, make sure your last look to a downhill hole is at the right side of the green and aim accordingly. Then pull the trigger. Conversely, if the hole plays significantly uphill, then make sure your last look is at the far left-hand side of the green because your vision will tend to get pulled to the right. If you make the proper adjustments with your eyes, you should hit the green every time.

# Tom Watson: Revisiting the Miracle Chip on No. 17

In the first four U.S. Opens contested at Pebble Beach, the par-3 17th hole played as the toughest hole relative to par, which is extremely rare for a par-3. The par-5 14th hole has always been the No. 1 handicap hole at Pebble Beach, but the back-left pin location from the U.S. Open tees (208 yards) makes the 17th a bear of a hole.

"It may be the smallest par-3 green for that length of hole that I've ever seen in my life," said Tom Watson, winner of the 1982 U.S. Open at Pebble Beach and five British Open championships. "It takes every bit of your skill to get the ball on that green."

The 17th hole is the scene of the most famous shot of Watson's storied career, and it didn't come hitting the green off the tee. Needing a birdie to forge ahead of Jack Nicklaus on the final day of the '82 U.S. Open, Watson's tee shot on No. 17 drifted into the lush rough, 16 feet from the cup. A par looked out of the question, but somehow Watson miraculously chipped in for birdie and a one-shot lead. He followed with a birdie on the par-5 18th for a two-shot win over Nicklaus.

As legend has it, caddie Bruce Edwards told Watson just as he was preparing to hit the shot, "to get the ball close." Watson responded by saying, "To hell with getting it close—I'm going to make it."

He did just that.

"That particular chip shot was a very short, downhill chip shot," recalled Watson. "I looked at it, and frankly, I thought to myself that if I could hit the pin I could stop the ball.

That was the logical thing to think about at that point: 'Take dead aim!' as Harvey Penick said. And I did. I knew it broke left. I aimed right of the hole...you never know how the ball is going to come out of the heavy rough, but it came out exactly the way I meant it to, which is softly, as high as I could hit it."

Watson's approach to that shot nearly three decades ago was very aggressive, but as he said, he had little other choice if he wanted to get the ball close. His advice to amateurs when facing a similar near-impossible shot or one they fear is to proceed with a little more caution and common sense.

"When you're faced with a situation like that, you have to understand the risk and reward of it," said Watson. "If there's a high risk factor, you try to keep your thoughts simple. Play to an area [of the green] that is maybe not your best outcome but is better than a poor outcome. It's hard to tell that to most golfers because of their egos; they think I'm going to play my absolute best shot right here. Well, that doesn't occur very often. You have to go with what you're capable of, understanding the next move, just as in chess. When you learn how to play golf that way, and you're consistently thinking about your next move with each shot that you play, then you have a good handle on how to play the game."

For more on how to handle the most feared shots at Pebble Beach and your home course, turn to Chapter 7.

**Tom Watson, seen here with longtime caddie Bruce Edwards, won the 1982 U.S. Open at Pebble Beach thanks to a miraculous chip-in for birdie on the par-3 17th hole.** William C. Brooks, PBC Archives

A short pitch over a greenside bunker, such as this one on the par-4 4th hole, is commonplace at Pebble Beach.

# Chapter 5

# Rules of the Short Game

U ntil February, when Monterey Peninsula Country Club replaced Poppy Hills, the three courses in the rotation for the Pebble Beach AT&T National Pro-Am were Pebble Beach, Poppy Hills, and Spyglass Hill. Of the three, Pebble Beach typically played the easiest (relative to par) for the tour professionals and Spyglass Hill the most difficult. Poppy Hills usually fell in the middle.

For the average golfer, however, Pebble Beach has always been the most challenging of the three courses because of the demands it places on your short game. The greens are exceptionally small, which makes them difficult to hit even from short distances. If you miss the green, you're likely pitching the ball up and over a bunker or playing from the bunker. Those are two shots that most recreational golfers aren't very good at; they don't have the skillset to hit the ball high and land it soft.

Spyglass Hill plays easier for the mid-handicapper because the greens are much bigger. Golfers can more or less play their regular game, which is to hit the ball in the fairway, land the approach shot just short of the green, pitch on, take two putts, and move on to the next hole. At Pebble Beach, one feels as if he's shooting at a dartboard from 50 yards away: if your distance control isn't perfect, you can find yourself in a bad situation. It's not uncommon to see golfers make a six or seven from inside

# Rules of the Short Game

**1. Investigate the Lie:** Examine the lie carefully, because it will determine which club to use and how big a swing to take.

**2. Take Lay of the Land:** As you walk up to the green, there are several important things to which you should pay attention, including the firmness and slope of the green.

**3. Minimum Air Time, Maximum Ground Time:** The safest shot around the green is the one that rolls the most and flies the least.

**4. Take a Dress Rehearsal:** After you've selected your club, follow the appropriate practice shot routine to lock in the right tempo for the shot.

**5. Chip with a Variety of Clubs:** Develop one swing but modify your carry-to-roll ratio by employing a variety of different clubs.

**6. Lose the Angles in Your Swing:** Minimize wrist hinge and alter the trajectory of your shots by going to a more- or less-lofted club.

**7. Follow Through to the Target:** Learn to make your follow through at least as long as your backswing to hit your ball the right distance with the right trajectory.

**8. Hover the Club at Address:** Use this technique to avoid overreaching—grounding the club at address—and chunking your chip shots.

**9. Maintain Constant Grip Pressure:** Grip your wedges more firmly than your longer irons.

100 yards, even if they're playing their third shot from the fairway. That's how Pebble Beach is. It confounds and exasperates you.

Pebble Beach requires you to hit a variety of different shots from inside 50 yards, depending on the direction the wind is blowing, how firm or soft the greens are, and several other factors. A perfect example of this is the par-5 6th hole, which is exposed on a bluff overlooking Stillwater Cove. When the hole is playing into the wind or a crosswind, it's best to play a low pitch or bump-and-run shot and keep the ball under the wind. If it's playing downwind, you'll want to hit a medium-trajectory ball short of the green and let it release on. If there's no wind whatsoever, then you can play a high-trajectory pitch shot (what most people would consider a normal pitch shot) and fly it all the way to the hole.

The conditions at Pebble Beach dictate that you play a variety of different short-game shots. Here, I'm demonstrating a low bump-and-run shot (photos 1 and 2) and a medium-trajectory pitch (photos 3 and 4) into the 6th green. The bump and run is an effective way to keep the ball under the wind.

In this chapter, I'll share with you a set of short-game rules and fundamentals that will help you hit every type of shot around the green and significantly reduce the amount of strokes you take inside 50 yards. If you follow these principles and refer back to them from time to time, you will be a much improved and more confident player around the greens.

## Rule No. 1: Investigate the Lie

Is the ball sitting up in the grass or down? Is the grass lying against you or away from you? The lie determines which club to use, because it dictates how much loft you require, what length of swing you take, and how much spin you're able to put on the ball.

For example, should you find yourself in the greenside rough at Pebble Beach with the ball sitting on top of the grass, you can play the shot like a normal chip and run (provided you have a reasonable amount of green to work with) with a 9-iron or pitching wedge and simply brush the grass. However, if the ball settles down in the ryegrass, which is very sticky, you have to take a more-lofted club and pinch the ball out of there using a steep, descending swing. At address, look at the front half of the ball, which will drop your lead shoulder to create a steeper plane. This helps you get the club through the turf a little easier.

## Rule No. 2: Take Lay of the Land

When you're approaching the green from a distance, take note of the following: is the green playing uphill or downhill? How much undulation is there to it? Which way is the green going to

Most of the greens at Pebble Beach—like No. 6 here—slope from back to front, but you can't tell how much from a distance. By walking up to the green, you'll see just how much it slopes and which way it breaks.

**Provided there are no obstacles between you and the flag, it's best to get the ball rolling on the ground as soon as possible.**

move your ball when it lands? As you get closer, try to determine whether the greens are firm or soft. Do the same with the area in front of the green. This information is crucial to hitting the ball close, especially if you're pitching from 40 or 50 yards away.

A lot of golfers don't pay attention to the area around the green unless it has a lip and a lot of sand in it. But if the fringe is playing soft, you might have a difficult time bouncing the ball through it, which means your best play will be to carry the ball onto the green. The slope of the green is also a crucial factor. Most of the greens at Pebble Beach slope from back to front toward the ocean. Hole No. 10 is a perfect example of this, and if you flirt too much with the right side of the green, you could be staring at a big number.

Another thing to pay attention to as you survey the green is the pin position. If the pin

is back, you want to leave your approach shot short of the flagstick and leave yourself an uphill putt. Conversely, if it's up front, make sure you carry the ball far enough on the green so it settles past the flagstick. You might have a quick putt going down the hill, but if you come up short, then you're likely chipping or pitching on again.

## Rule 3: Minimum Air Time, Maximum Ground Time

The simplest, safest shot around the green is the one that rolls the most. If you have no bunkers or other obstacles you have to carry, then get the ball rolling on the ground as soon as possible. The ball will hold its line better and have less opportunity to stray off-line than it would if you tried to fly it all the way to the hole. At least you know where it's headed

## Understanding How Bounce Works

The most important feature on your wedges (and perhaps in the entire short game) is bounce, which we defined earlier as the angle between the leading edge of the clubhead and the ground. The greater the bounce, the easier time you have gliding the clubhead through the sand.

The best golfers in the world understand this and have no fear when it comes to hitting out of a greenside bunker. They know exactly how deep a divot they want to create and how much sand they want to move. If they draw

a nice lie in the bunker or the sand is very fluffy, they'll open the clubface some and expose the bounce so the clubhead won't dig too much. Conversely, if the ball is plugged or the sand is very firm, they'll square or even close the clubface to encourage it to dig.

One other thing the pro knows is that it takes a lot of sand to propel the ball out of

the bunker. The average golfer is afraid to touch the sand and tries to help the ball up and out of the bunker. The pro, on the other hand, is not hitting the ball; he's hitting the sand. The compression of the strike projects the sand forward, along with the ball.

It takes a little practice, but if you want to get the ball out of the bunker every time, you have to make a descending blow and feel as if you're tossing the sand onto the green. Set up to the ball as you normally would for a pitch shot of the same distance—ball centered, weight left, shoulders square to the target and as level as you can make them. Open the clubface slightly, and make a 10 (o'clock) to 2 swing with your arms, keeping your weight on your forward leg. The club is going to meet some resistance from the sand, so make sure you accelerate the club into a fairly full finish. Because you're moving the sand and not the ball, the distance you have to cover from the bunker is going to be greater than a pitch of the same length. Practice these fundamentals for an hour each week, and you should start having as much fun in the sand as the pros do.

**The bounce refers to the angle between the leading edge of the clubhead and the ground (inset). It helps the clubhead glide through the sand, so you can take a nice, shallow divot under the ball and splash the right amount of sand out of the bunker.**

when it's rolling out. If you need to hit a 56- or 60-degree club, then you've put yourself in a tough position to make par because you have to stop the ball with trajectory or spin and manufacture a bigger swing. Any golfer can make a putting or chipping stroke, but few are comfortable making a partial or full swing so close to the green.

If you find yourself having to pitch over a bunker, find the safest route onto the green. It might be that you're pitching 20 or 30 feet away from the flag, but it's better to leave two putts and move onto the next hole than attempt a shot you haven't practiced before. As long as your first shot lands on the green, you have a chance of making a 20- or 25-footer and perhaps walking away with par.

## Rule 4: Take a Dress Rehearsal

Make several rehearsal swings off to the side of the ball and brush the turf where the ball would be relative to your stance. Then, using the same tempo grooved in your rehearsal swings, step up to the ball and hit the shot. Don't waste any more time thinking about club selection or the amount of loft you want to produce; you should have done that already. The best short-game players in the world establish a rhythm for the type of shot they want to hit, and once they find it, they step up to the ball and execute with confidence—without any concern for the outcome.

If, after surveying the green, you're still unsure of the distance and how hard you should hit the shot, make three rehearsal swings: one that is clearly too big, a second that is too small, and a third in the middle. The last rehearsal

**Depending on the amount of carry and roll required, you can chip with everything from your putter to a hybrid.**

swing is the one you want to put into play. Once you've established that "middle" rhythm, go up and brush the grass. Don't concern yourself with the ball; brush the turf and let the ball get in the way of the swinging clubhead.

Make sure to look at the target as you make your rehearsal swings. By connecting with the target, you'll direct your energy toward it, accelerating the clubhead through to the finish. Golfers who struggle with short-game shots typically freeze at impact; their body stops pivoting, and the club runs out of gas at the ball. The body must continue to move with the club through the shot to strike the ball solidly.

## Rule 5: Chip with a Variety of Clubs

I talked earlier about the importance of keeping the ball on the ground as much as possible. The way to do that on longer chips is to use a variety of different clubs. The best player in the world, Tiger Woods, employs everything from a 4-iron to a pitching wedge when playing a long chip or bump-and-run shot. He uses his normal reverse-overlap putting grip, picks out a spot just over the fringe where he wants the ball to land, and makes a descending swing into the back of the ball. It's very similar to a putting stroke with a little more backswing to it.

The amount of carry and roll you obtain with this method is determined by the degree of loft on the club. The less loft you use, the shorter the ball will carry in the air and the farther it will roll out and vice versa. A pitching wedge will typically roll twice as far as it flies in the air; thus, it will have a carry-to-roll ratio of 1:2. A 9-iron will have a ratio of 1:3, an 8-iron 1:4, and so on. There's a lot of numbers to keep track of, but just remember, if you want maximum roll and distance, use a longer club.

What's helpful about this method of chipping is that it requires only one swing, and the ball reacts similarly off the clubface, no matter which club you use. The more you become acquainted with the amount of roll each club produces, the better your distance control and scoring will be around the greens.

## Rule 6: Lose the Angles in Your Swing

The short game is all about distance control: you don't need to generate a lot of clubhead

**Short-game shots require very little power; therefore, keep your wrist hinge to a minimum (photo 2). Change trajectories by switching to a more- or less-lofted club, and by moving your ball position forward (for higher shots) or back (for lower shots).**

Rules of the Short Game    **63**

speed or power to hit the ball 50 yards, unless you're playing from U.S. Open-length rough. It's for this reason that I recommend you keep the angles in your swing to a minimum on most finesse shots.

By angles, I'm referring to the angle created by your left forearm (on right-handed golfers) and clubshaft when you hinge your wrists upward in the backswing, or the forward lean to the shaft you produce when you place the ball back in your stance or push your hands too far forward. Once you create these angles, you have to get rid of them at some point in your swing. That can be very difficult for an amateur to master in the short distance the clubhead travels on a chip or pitch shot.

If you want to keep the ball low, then bring the trajectory down by switching to a less-lofted club, like a pitching wedge or 9-iron. You only need to play the ball slightly back of center in your stance for these shots; the loft on the club will do the rest. The same is true when you want to hit a high, soft pitch shot: choose your highest-lofted wedge (56 or 60 degrees) and position the ball slightly forward of center in your stance, so the handle is in line with the leading edge of the clubface.

Many golfers set up to play a high pitch shot with the ball back in their stance, sometimes off their big toe. This introduces the leading edge of the club, resulting in it digging too much. All wedges have a feature called bounce, which by definition is the angle between the leading and trailing edges on the club's sole. The more bounce a club has, the less likely it is to dig into the turf or sand. By not leaning the club so far forward, you expose the bounce and create a much greater margin for error.

## Rule 7: Follow Through to the Target

There are two factors that determine the length of a shot: 1) the length of your swing and 2) the speed at which you swing the club. When I refer

**Follow through to the target on partial shots, as if you were pitching horseshoes at the flagstick.**

to the length of the swing, I'm speaking as much to the forward swing as I am the backswing. Your follow-through should be at least as long as your backswing to hit the ball the right distance with the right trajectory. Most golfers take a long backswing and then decelerate into impact with a shorter follow-through because their minds are telling them they've made too big a swing for such a short shot.

The golf swing is a circle, and a circle has symmetry to it. If you think about tossing horseshoes, you always pitch them with a similar-length backswing and forward swing. You should approach all short-game shots the same way. This allows you to generate enough speed on both sides of the ball to propel it the required distance. As the arms swing forward, the body is going to turn, or pivot, to help them out, which will keep the acceleration more constant throughout the swing.

Practice hitting partial shots to get a feel for the length of swing (both back and through) required to hit the ball 20, 30, 40 yards, and so on. For example: take your sand wedge and swing your arms back to 8 o'clock (just above knee height for most golfers) and then follow through to 4 o'clock; that should produce a shot of 20 yards every time. The same-length backswing with a slightly longer follow-through (to 3 o'clock) will produce a 30-yard shot. A 2 o'clock follow-through with just a little faster body rotation will create a 40-yard shot. In a sense, you can control the distance more with your follow-through than your backswing. But you've got to let your swing develop on both sides of the ball; that is the key.

## Tom Watson: Practice the High Lob

When Tom Watson was just 11 years old, his longtime teacher and mentor, Stan Thirsk, had him practicing from all types of bad lies and trouble areas around the green. One shot he taught Watson was the high lob, which comes in handy around Pebble Beach because of how easy it is to shortside yourself. The greens are so small at Pebble Beach that if you misfire just a little bit, you may find yourself with a short, delicate pitch over a bunker with little green to work with.

"My favorite drill is the high, soft shot, where you open the face up about 45 degrees, aim left about 45 degrees, take the club way to the outside, and cut inside and across the ball," said Watson. "The ball will catch just a little part of the clubhead and shoot straight up in the air, very softly."

Most golfers don't know how to hit this shot safely because they've never practiced it, according to Watson. The only time they see it is out on the course, and by then, they're cooked because they don't know how to execute it properly. Like most short-game shots, the key is to make sure you accelerate the clubhead through impact and into the finish.

"It's a shot that really helped my short game," Watson said. "I learned how to hit the ball high and soft with a hard swing."

# Tom Kite: Acceleration Is Key on Partial Wedge Shots

Widely considered to be one of the greatest wedge players of all time, Tom Kite says the key to knocking down the flag inside 60 yards is exercising good distance control.

"It's all about feeling the distance, feeling the touch, being able to make solid contact, and making the ball go the right distance," said Kite. "Everybody hits it reasonably straight from 30 yards. They may hit the ball 30 yards past the hole or chunk it right in front of them, but they're not going to hit it 30 yards off-line."

The reason amateurs struggle to make the ball go the right distance on partial wedge shots is that they don't know how to throttle down their clubhead speed, says Kite.

"You see them swing the club back way too long and fast," explained Kite. "There's way too much speed and length and consequently they have to decelerate the club. We all know the club is more stable when it's accelerating. That acceleration is the key to every shot, whether it's a two-inch putt, a 40- or 50-yard wedge shot or a 300-yard drive. The club has to be accelerating. Now, having said that, it doesn't have to be accelerating fast, but it has to be accelerating."

Kite recommends amateurs shorten and slow down their backswings, so they have no choice but to accelerate the club on their forward swings. He points to the long, languid flop-shot swings of Phil Mickelson and Fred Couples, which are exceedingly slow but accelerating through impact.

"If you need to have a swing that's moving at 20 miles per hour, well you'd better not have a backswing that's traveling 30 miles per hour; otherwise, you couldn't accelerate it to 20," says Kite. "You'd have to slow it down. You have to learn how to accelerate the club to make the shot go the required distance."

## Rule 8: Hover the Club at Address

When you set up to the ball, extend your arms as long as you can so the leading edge of the club is just below the equator, or center, of the golf ball. When you swing, the weight of the club should stretch your arms out even more so the clubhead finds the bottom of the golf ball and

**Suspend the clubhead in the air so it's just below the center of the golf ball (opposite page), with your arms fully extended (above). This will promote a smoother takeaway and more crisp contact.**

makes solid contact with it. Another advantage to suspending the clubhead in the air is that it won't stub the grass going back, thereby giving your swing a greater sense of freedom.

The gentleman who taught me this method of underreaching was Paul Runyan, one of greatest short-game players and teachers ever. The problem with overreaching, or grounding the club at address, is that when the arms straighten out, the clubhead goes straight into the ground. This is why you see amateurs chunk their chips and pitches a lot.

Hovering the club will all but ensure that the clubhead will bottom out on the target side of the ball, not before the ball, which is the key to making crisp contact.

## Rule 9: Maintain Constant Grip Pressure

Your wedges are the heaviest clubs in your bag, so make sure you grip these clubs more tightly than you would your driver or longer irons. Once you have the club secure, keep your grip pressure constant throughout the swing. Many amateurs soften up their grip pressure when they swing into impact because they're trying to be too delicate with the shot; some even let go of the club. If you're real uptight about a certain shot, grip the club tighter, especially if you have to hit a lofted shot over a bunker or some other hazard. By gripping the club a little firmer, you'll be less inclined to let the club go and more likely to hit the ball solidly.

A good putter can erase a lot of sins on the golf course and make you much more confident in your full swing as well.

# Chapter 6

# Your Putter as an Eraser

The 2000 U.S. Open at Pebble Beach will go down as one of the greatest ever. Not only did it mark the 100th edition of our national championship, but it was Jack Nicklaus' 44th and final U.S. Open start, one he punctuated by reaching the par-5 18th hole in two shots with a 3-wood from 260 yards. But what it will be most remembered for is Tiger Woods' virtuoso performance. In what felt like a symbolic passing of the torch from Nicklaus to Woods, Tiger lapped the field by a record 15 shots, tying the lowest 72-hole score (12 under) in a U.S. Open and smashing several other records along the way.

When the dismantling of the field was over, an awed Nick Price was quoted as saying, "We always felt someone would come along who could drive the ball 300 yards and putt like Ben Crenshaw. This guy drives the ball farther than anybody I've ever seen and putts better than Crenshaw."

Woods' entire game was on that week, but if one particular area stood out, it was his putting. On the eve before the first round, Woods spent hours on the practice green working on his posture and release. And did it ever pay off! Woods needed only 24 putts in an opening-round 65 and didn't record a single three-putt all week. Time and time again Tiger stared down a critical par-saving putt and sank it. His bogey-free final round of 67 started with nine consecutive par putts before he rattled off four birdies in the next five holes.

# Laird's Lessons

## Using Your Putter as an Eraser

**1. How to Build a Repeatable Stroke:** The key to good putting is distance control, and the key to distance control is swinging your putterhead at a consistent pace, like a pendulum.

**2. Right-Hand-Only Drill:** Use this technique to help gain awareness for the pacing and feel of your putting stroke.

**3. Practice to a Target, Not a Hole:** Try these drills to develop distance control and build confidence in consistently leaving long putts close to the hole.

**4. Lag Putts—Proceed with Caution:** Take the same approach as the pros on putts of 30 feet or longer, playing conservatively with the goal being a gimme second putt.

**5. Use Your Feet as a Guide:** Follow the lead of blind golfer Tom Sullivan and learn to read putts with your feet.

**6. Short Putts—Throw a Spare:** This bowling analogy will help you hit your short putts firmly enough to keep them on-line and in the hole.

**7. "Pick It Up, It's Good":** Follow Paul Azinger's advice and stay relaxed and confident on testy short putts.

**8. Linear vs. Nonlinear:** Golfers tends to see putts in one of two ways; it's important to determine how your eyes view things.

**9. Green Reading Basics:** Use this brief primer to confidently determine the line of your putt.

**10. Local Knowledge:** A golf course's location always influences putting. Find somebody who knows the course, and get their advice.

---

In his press conference following the record-setting performance, Woods talked about how important all those par-saving putts were to sustaining and building upon the momentum he had. This is what a hot putter can do for you. I like to call it the "big eraser" because it can correct a lot of sins. You may not be hitting the ball particularly well one day, but you can still get it around in very few strokes if you're putting well. The opposite is also true, however: if you're three-putting a lot of greens, you're not going to score well, regardless of how perfectly you're hitting the ball.

Putting is the most precise part of the game, because the target is the smallest. The hole is just 4¼ inches in diameter; your average fairway is about 35 yards wide. That doesn't leave you with much margin for error, nor does it allow for a fragile state of confidence. There are some very important mechanics that need to be adhered to in putting to be successful, but your mind and preparation are just as important,

**Tiger Woods' masterful putting was key to his record-setting 15-stroke victory at the 2000 U.S. Open at Pebble Beach.** Photo courtesy Getty Images

probably more so. In this chapter, I will share some practices and lessons from the game's best putters that will have you holing more putts and three-putting a lot less.

# 1. How to Build a Repeatable Stroke

The average length of the first putt for most golfers is around 35 feet, certainly not "gimme" two-putt range. To get the ball close enough for an easy tap-in, you must exercise good distance control. If you can consistently hit your putts at the correct speed and distance, you'll two-putt a lot more than you three-putt, and you'll even make the occasional putt or two.

Just how do you practice good distance control? The first thing you must do is learn how to swing the putterhead at a consistent pace, similar to how a pendulum operates. A pendulum swings under the influence of gravity, and therefore its forward momentum remains constant. If you can get the element of time to be repeatable in your stroke, the putterhead will start to deliver the same amount of energy to the ball and produce the same consistent roll. This, in turn, will allow you to judge the speed and break better and read the greens more effectively.

The best players in the world have a steady beat, or tempo, to their stroke, which is why they're able to control their distances so well. There's no overacceleration or slowing down of the putterhead through impact. It's always "one-two, back-hit." The ratio of backswing to forward swing is 1:2, because the forward swing is twice as long. But the time it takes to swing the putterhead back and then into impact is exactly the same (1:1). It remains the same cadence regardless of how short or long the stroke is; the putterhead might travel a greater distance, but it's getting to the ball in the same amount of time.

Where amateurs struggle is when they either outrace that clock by making the putterhead move too quickly, or they slow it down (in this case they've made too big of a backswing). Good putters only slow the putter down after it has collided with the ball, which is why their follow-through appears abbreviated.

Practice putting to a cadence and, should you find your rhythm getting disrupted on the course, take three practice swings by the side of ball: one that you know is too long and would cause the ball to run through the break, one that is too short and will leave you with a lengthy second putt, and one in the middle. Use the swing in the middle and hit the putt.

Another way to practice is by putting with a device known as a metronome. The metronome is a timing instrument that helps players establish a repeatable beat, or rhythm, to their stroke. The average beat for a PGA TOUR player is 76 beats per minute, or eight-tenths of a second. Using this device on a repeatable basis, a player will learn to groove a consistent rhythm to his stroke, which is eight-tenths of a second going back and another eight-tenths of a second swinging into impact. Provided the beat is the same, the rate of acceleration will be a constant speed, which allows you to make solid contact and control your distance.

## 2. Right-Hand-Only Drill

This is the best putting drill I know to help you gain awareness for the pacing of your stroke. When you warm up prior to your round, putt with your right hand only. Start about 30 feet away from your target and hit five balls as close to the target as possible. Gradually move closer to the target and repeat the drill. Notice how the putterhead swings, how it moves in an unforced motion back and through, and how light your grip pressure is. This is the same kind of feel you want to have with both hands on the club.

Putting one-handed encourages you to swing the club—not guide it or overaccelerate it toward the target—so there is a solid collision between the putterface and the ball. It's easier to keep your hands relaxed so you can gain awareness for what a solid, repeatable strike feels like. With two hands, the tendency is for one hand to overtake the other and either swing the putter too fast or too slow.

**Putting with one hand teaches you to release the putterhead, not guide it toward the hole.**

## 3. Practice to a Target, Not a Hole

Prior to hitting the first tee box, take a few balls to the middle of the practice green and stroke each one as close to the fringe as possible without putting them off the green. If you can't go at the fringe, find a discoloration on the green or some other mark you can putt at. Focus on rolling the ball along the green and stopping it close to your target.

Hit a few additional putts like this with your right hand only, and then again with both hands, getting a feel for the speed of the greens and how much the slope is moving the ball. Make sure to vary each putt so you're hitting some uphill, downhill, and sidehill. Once you have a good awareness for the speed of the greens, find a hole and hit a few short putts, listening for the sound of the ball rattling around at the bottom of the cup.

The reason why you should ignore the hole for so long is because when you putt to a hole, the focus becomes making the putt instead of hitting the ball the correct distance. Your preround focus should be on speed and distance, nothing else. The problem with dropping a few balls down at 15 or 20 feet and putting them to a hole, as most amateurs do, is that they rarely go in. That doesn't help build confidence, nor does it give you much indication for the speed of the greens. Most three-putts are a result of the first putt not being the right distance; practice your distance control and finish your warm-up with a few confidence-building short putts, and you'll be good to go.

## 4. Lag Putts: Proceed with Caution

As I stated earlier, the average length of most first putts is 35 feet. From this distance, assuming a relatively flat or uphill putt, most tour pros would expect to get the ball within a foot and a half to two feet of the hole or approximately a 10-percent radius of the hole (equal to a three-and-a-half-foot diameter circle around the hole). If the putt is downhill, a little sidehill, or has quite a bit of break to it, it's less of a green-light situation. In this instance, they're just trying to get the ball close enough to the hole to leave themselves a reasonable

**As part of your pre-putt routine, take several practice strokes behind your ball, perpendicular to the hole (photo 1). Assume your setup and take one last look at your target (photo 2)—which, in most cases, is the point at which your ball starts breaking toward the hole—and swing (photo 3).**

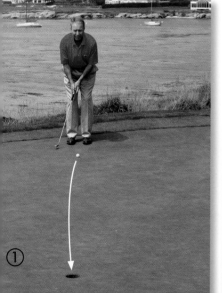

①

②

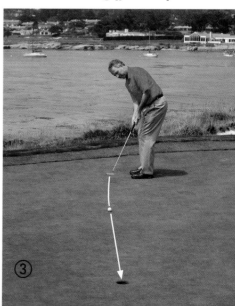

③

chance of two-putting. The one thing they don't want to do is give a shot away to the course; they would rather have the course take it away from them. If they hit the putt with the right amount of speed and it goes in, that's wonderful; otherwise, they take two putts and go on to the next hole.

Take a cue from the best players in the world and on putts of 30 feet or longer, proceed with caution (yellow-light approach). Your goal is to leave your second putt within gimme range; if the first one happens to roll in, consider it a bonus. Go back to the pre-round practice drill I discussed earlier and focus on hitting the putt the correct distance and nothing else. On the course, forget about the hole; instead, stand behind your ball, perpendicular to the hole, so both eyes are looking straight ahead on your line, and make two or three rehearsal swings to feel the amount of energy necessary to hit the ball the proper distance. Walk around to your

ball, place your putter behind it, and then take one last look at your target for confirmation. If the putt is breaking two feet from right to left, then that last look should be at a spot a few feet above the hole and not the hole. Once you have your target in mind, return your eyes back to the ball and make your stroke. Don't take too much time over the ball because you're likely to disrupt the feeling you have for the rhythm of your stroke.

## 5. Use Your Feet as a Guide

One of my good friends, singer, author, and producer Tom Sullivan, is one of the best lag putters I know. Rarely do I see him three-putt from 30 feet or beyond. What makes that so extraordinary is that Tom is blind. He's been blind his entire life and has never seen the beauty and splendor of Pebble Beach. But he can feel it. When we play, Tom takes my arm, and we walk the entire length of the putt, from

**You can calibrate the length of each putt using your feet as a guide. Take your stance so each big toe is separated by the width of your putter's grip (photo 2), and swing from toe to toe (photos 1 and 3). That should produce a putt of six feet; for longer putts, swing to the outside of both feet and so on.**

his ball to the hole and back again. During that time, Tom reads the putt with his feet. This not only gives him a feel for the putt's distance but also whether the green slopes from left to right or right to left and if it's uphill or downhill. Once he's programmed the distance, speed, and break in his mind, he dials up a certain-length stroke that he knows will produce the desired length he's seeking.

Through many hours of practice, Tom has learned to associate various-length strokes with certain distances. You can learn this association method, too. Take your stance so that your two big toes are separated by the width of your putter grip (all grips are the same length). From this position, swing the putterhead from big toe to big toe, maintaining the same rhythm on your backswing and forward stroke ("one Mississippi, two Mississippi"). On a completely flat surface, this length of stroke should produce a putt of about six feet. Next, swing the putterhead to the outside of both feet (roughly a 12-foot putt), then to the creases on each pant leg (18 feet), and finally the outside of both thighs (36 feet). It's very similar to using the hands on a clockface to gauge the distance of your pitch shots. Once you have the stroke and distance calibrated, you can adjust the length of the stroke based on the slope of the green. For example, if you have a six-foot putt that's slightly uphill, you know to swing the putterhead back a little past your big toe because the putt is going to be slower and vice versa if the putt is downhill.

## 6. Short Putts—Throw a Spare

Probably the most challenging green to putt at Pebble Beach is No. 13, because it has the most

tilt to it. But unless you're putting from above the hole, you want to be much more aggressive on putts inside five feet than on those from 30 feet. The reason is simple: you want these short putts to hold their line, and that requires a firm stroke. If you hit the putt too tentatively, it's likely to take on too much break and either lip out of the cup or slide by the edge.

When you have these putts, imagine you're bowling, and the lone pin between you and a spare is directly in front of the hole. To get the ball in the hole, you need to hit your putt with enough pace to knock the pin down. Another great image on short putts is to pretend there's a backboard behind the hole: pick a discoloration or piece of grass at the back of the cup and hit your putt right at that spot with enough speed to

On short putts, imagine there's a tee in front of the hole and it's all that's standing between you and a spare. Knock the tee down and the ball will find its way into the cup.

bank the ball in. So long as you remain committed to your line and keep the putterhead traveling toward the target, you should see—and hear—a lot more short putts drop.

## 7. "Pick It Up, It's Good"

I received an emergency phone call from one of my students just prior to the start of the 2000 AT&T Pebble Beach National Pro-Am. Apparently he had played his final practice round in preparation for the Pro-Am and was having trouble making anything inside six feet. I told him to come on over, and we met on the putting green outside my office at Spyglass Hill.

After watching him hit a few putts, I realized there was nothing technically wrong with his stroke. I could only assume he had missed a few short putts during his practice round, maybe because of some bumps on the greens, and had lost his confidence. While I was giving him a lesson, Paul Azinger had been observing what was going on and asked if he could jump in and share some advice. Paul had won the Hawaiian Open a few months earlier and had found this tip—which he learned from noted sports psychologist Bob Rotella—very helpful. He said, "When you've got a two- or three-footer to finish a hole, don't your buddies always say to you, 'Go ahead, pick it up, it's good'? And what do you always do?" My guy says, "Well, I kind of halfway slap it at the hole, and it almost always goes in." Paul said, "Isn't it amazing how that happens?"

Paul's advice to my student was this: The next time you have a six-footer or a testy short putt, assume the putt is good. Before you make your stroke, say to yourself, "Pick it up, it's good" and bring that same relaxed attitude to your stroke. If your intention is to make it ("It's good"), your mind is freed up to allow for a nice, positive stroke. With Paul's help, my guy was able to regain his confidence on these short putts and enjoy some success in the tournament.

## 8. Linear vs. Nonlinear

Before I discuss green reading, it's important that you know whether you're a linear or nonlinear putter. Linear putters see every putt as a straight putt, whether it has some break to it or not; they look for the high point of the putt and hit the ball straight at this point, allowing for gravity to swing the ball toward the hole. As the putt is slowing down, the slope takes over and curves the ball toward the hole.

Nonlinear putters see the putt as a curved track. First, they determine where they want the ball to enter the cup (some find it helpful to view the hole as a clockface, with 6 o'clock being straight on; 7, 8, 9, and 10 o'clock to the left; and 5, 4, 3, and 2 o'clock to the right), and then their eyes trace a path from the hole back to the ball. The nonlinear putter is more concerned with the starting point—where do I need to start the ball in order for it to take the right amount of break?—than the linear putter is. The line is predicated on where the ball is entering the hole and at what speed.

## 9. Green Reading Basics

Besides being very small, Pebble Beach greens are also relatively flat. There doesn't appear to be a lot of slope to them, but the slopes they do have are very subtle. You need to pay close attention to the area around each hole because that's where the movement tends to be greatest. The greens also slope toward the ocean, which isn't evident when you're standing right over your putt. For example, on the first hole, you'd swear the green slopes from right to left, but it does exactly the opposite. If you looked at the green from 30 yards away you'd see this, but if you wait until you're on the putting surface to assess the break, you've put yourself at a disadvantage.

Start reading the green from 30 yards away, as you're walking up to it. This is the first step in reading greens properly. From this perspective,

**The best place to read a putt is midway between your ball and the hole, on the low side of the putt.**

you should be able to see which way the green is tilted and whether it's uphill or downhill. Most greens will look uphill because they're sloped from back to front to allow for the water to drain off; very rarely do they slope from front to back.

When you do get to the green, look for the fall line, which is the straightest path the water will take (through the hole) as it's draining off the green. If you're left of the fall line, your putt is going to break to the right, and if you're right of it, it will break to the left. Determine where the low side of the putt is and walk to this side—midway between your ball and the hole. This will give you the best view of the entire putt and will magnify any break you see. Walk a few more paces toward the hole and observe the area around the cup where your ball will be traveling on the last few feet of its journey. Determine where you want the ball to enter the cup, keeping in mind that the putt is going to break most around the hole, as it's slowing down considerably.

If, at this point, you're still unsure of the line, walk to the other side of the hole and get a look from behind the hole. Make sure you're committed to your line before you get over your putt; otherwise you're more likely to change your mind at the last second, which will only

sabotage your efforts. If you're one of the last players to putt in your group, go to school on your playing companions' putts: How's the speed? How much is his or her putt breaking? What's it doing around the hole? If one of them is chipping or pitching on, watch their ball run out toward the hole. The more information you can use to validate your read, the better chance you have of holing the putt.

## 10. Local Knowledge

As I mentioned earlier, the Pebble Beach greens tend to slope toward the ocean, which is very helpful information when you're unsure of how a putt might break. For those of you who have played golf in Scottsdale, you know that putts generally break away from Pinnacle Peak toward the city of Phoenix. In South Florida, the grain grows toward the setting sun.

The location of a golf course can certainly influence the outcome of a putt, so if you're unfamiliar with the greens and you're playing a course that's near a large body of water or mountain range, don't be afraid to ask the pro if there's a pattern to the greens' movement. Chances are, the pro has played the course many times, and he'll clue you in on this valuable information.

A view from the behind the 8th hole, looking back at the big chasm that separates the upper fairway from the green.

# Chapter 7

# How to Overcome Fear on the Course

I f you're playing Pebble Beach Golf Links for the first time, chances are you already know about the tee shots on holes 7 and 18, the forced carry over the ocean on No. 8, and the downhill, sidehill approach shot on No. 10 toward Carmel Bay. The anticipation of hitting these shots is as great as playing the course, because you've seen them countless times before in pictures and on television.

The anticipation of playing these shots only stokes your level of anxiety. Coupled with the natural surroundings, smallish greens, and many hazards the architect has thrust at you, it's easy to become rattled by Pebble Beach.

We all have shots we fear, whether they are forced carries over water, long bunker shots, short bunker shots, or tee shots with out of bounds nearby. We fear them because we haven't had a great deal of success with them in the past, or we're afraid of the outcome. It's hard not to think about the ocean on No. 8, even if you can't see it, because you know it's there—just as you know it's lurking to the left of the tee on No. 18 and to the right of the green on No. 10.

How do you overcome this fear? As you'll learn in this chapter, it has as much to do with your attitude, preparation, and ability to stay calm and focused as it does your swing. What follows is a list of the 10 most-feared

# 10 Most-Feared Shots at Pebble Beach

**1. Second Shot on No. 8:** Know exactly how far it is to clear the hazard, and swing more club than is necessary.

**2. Tee Shot on No. 18:** One of the world's great tee shots offers a useful lesson applicable to any hole with trouble running tight to the fairway—put away your driver.

**3. Second Shot on No. 6:** Long, uphill, blind shots like this one require a different strategy than most approach shots.

**4. Tee Shot on No. 7:** Easy? Not for the average golfer. Learn how to deal with multiple challenges on short par-3s, including between-club distances, tricky winds, and distracting scenery.

**5. Tee Shot on No. 1:** The first shot on a famous course is always a tough one

mentally. Here are some tips to calm you down and get your round started right.

**6: Third Shot on No. 18:** The shot is short, but there are hazards everywhere. Determining the precise yardage is your first step to success.

**7. Pitch over Greenside Bunker on No. 14:** An uphill shot over a huge greenside bunker requires a different approach than a flat pitch, including planning for your possible mistakes.

**8. Left Greenside Bunker Shot on No. 7:** This busy bunker tests your mettle with a high lip and ocean water staring you in the face.

**9. Downhill, Sidehill Approach Shot on No. 10:** Awkward lies like this demand that you focus on balance and plan for the inevitable curve to the right.

**10. Long Bunker Shot on No. 17:** Here's how to get plenty of distance out of the sand trap—but not so much that you end up out in the ocean.

shots at Pebble Beach, based on my many years of observing golfers on the course as both a caddie and teacher. Almost all of these shots are present in one form or another on the courses you play. They may not have the Pacific Ocean as a water hazard, but every course has forced carries, sidehill lies, and bunkers. The tips in this chapter will help you be better prepared and more confident the next time you're standing over a trouble shot or a situation that makes you uneasy.

## 1. Second Shot on No. 8

A strong 3-wood on this hole will leave you with a mid-iron approach of about 170 yards, 120 yards of which is all carry over the ocean. But to the average golfer, that 120 yards seems like 220 yards; the distance appears much farther than it actually is. Any time you have a forced carry, find out the exact yardage you need to clear the hazard. If you know the carry is only 125 yards versus, say, 175 yards, you'll be more confident and

To reach the fairway below on the 8th hole, you must hit your approach over a deep oceanic chasm, 120 yards of which is all-carry.

relaxed, which will free up your muscles to make a more fluid swing.

So much of the fear on No. 8 is self-imposed. In your head you're thinking, "I don't want to go right because the ocean is there." So what happens? You grip the club a little tighter, leave the clubface open, and slice the ball to the right, into the ocean. Or you try so hard not to hit the ball to the right that you spin out early with your shoulders, come over the top, and hit a slice to the right. It's not all that different from a skier who tries to steer his skis by turning his shoulders instead of pointing his skis down the mountain and turning with the edges.

At some point, you have to allow the club to swing and just let it go. Think of a word that will help reduce the tension in your body and allow you to swing free and easy. For example, how many Os can you put in the word *smoooooooooooth*? Take more club than you think is necessary—i.e., a 5-iron or 4-hybrid vs. a

6-iron—so you don't try to get any extra distance out of the shot. You'll have more trust in the longer club, which will allow you to make a smooth three-quarter swing and hit the ball solidly.

If you're not sure you can cover the distance, choose a target that requires you to cover a smaller chunk of the forced carry. On No. 8, you can opt to go left of the chasm, which would leave an approach of about 80–100 yards, or you could take dead aim at the glove-shaped bunker short and left of the green. If you hit the ball straight, you've got a short pitch into the green, and if you hit the shot a little to the right, you just may end up on the green. Many times, amateurs try to hit shots that their skill set will not allow. If you don't think you can carry the ball over the chasm and onto the green—or very close to the green—at least six times out of 10, then don't try the shot. Find a shorter, safer route, pitch the ball on, two-putt, and walk away with your bogey.

However, if you're on vacation or playing the course for the first time, and you're just out to enjoy yourself, then go ahead and hit it. What's the worst that can happen? So you hit your shot into the ocean. Big deal—at least you tried it. Nothing about golf is stressful. It's you who adds the stress or fear. Many players look at this shot as a challenge and one that's fun to hit. They can't wait to get to it. Play with the same attitude, and you'll enjoy more success.

## 2. Tee Shot on No. 18

What few people know is how close Tiger Woods came to not winning the 2000 U.S. Open, which seems ridiculous considering he won by 15 shots. But after coming out early Saturday morning to finish his second round, Tiger hit a double-cross and hooked his tee shot on No. 18 into the ocean. When he went to tee the ball up again, his caddie, Steve

Williams, asked him if he was sure he wanted to hit driver again. What Steve knew and Tiger didn't was that it was his last ball. As it turns out, Tiger pulled a few balls out of his bag at the house where he was staying to practice chipping, and he left them there. He resumed his second round with only two balls in his golf bag, and had he hit his tee shot on 18 into the water, he would have been disqualified.

Tiger wound up finding the fairway with his second tee shot and posting a bogey.

Many golfers have left No. 18 with fewer balls than they started with. What makes this shot so scary, besides the fact that the ocean is right in front of you, is that for the first 13 driving holes at Pebble Beach you're asked to draw the ball, and if you overcook it here, you're in the ocean. Hit it too far to the right and you may wind up out of bounds. You also have to challenge the left side of the fairway to have any chance at making

**Many pros, including Tiger Woods, will hit iron off the tee on the par-5 18th and play it as a three-shot hole.**

birdie, and from the tee, there doesn't seem to be much room between the two trees in the center of the fairway and the ocean.

The wise play here is to put the driver away—as Tiger did during the final round of that U.S. Open (he hit a 4-iron; see Chapter 2)—and hit something that won't reach the two trees, like a 3-wood or rescue club. This will leave you in the widest part of the fairway, between the two fairway bunkers on the right, about 300 yards from the flag. Can you cover 300 yards in four shots for your par? Certainly you can. Whenever you have out of bounds left or right of you off the tee, hit a club you have confidence in, one you can swing aggressively without any fear of hitting a slice or, in this case, a hook. Look for the widest part of the fairway, which is the most conservative target, and let 'er rip.

## 3. Second Shot on No. 6

During the second round of the 2000 U.S. Open, Woods hit a blind, 7-iron approach from the deep ryegrass on this uphill par-5 to about 15 feet, prompting NBC analyst Roger Maltbie to utter the famous line, "This is not a fair fight." Tiger had to go over a tree, which is what prompted him to hit such a high-lofted club.

Tiger's approach was from 202 yards; naturally, most golfers will have a much longer second shot into this green, usually from a tightly mown fairway lie. Fear takes many forms on this shot: the ocean looms to the right, the fairway slopes hard from left to right, and it's a blind shot. Because it plays significantly uphill and the club of choice is usually a long, low-lofted club, the tendency is to try to help the ball up into the air. That's disaster. So many of these shots are either topped into the hill or lost to the ocean on the right because the golfer hangs back and tries to lift the ball.

Whenever you find yourself hitting an uphill approach like this one, or you fear you might top the ball, feel as if your weight is more on your forward leg and your left shoulder is lower than your right at address, which will help you to hit down on the ball. Make a few rehearsal swings,

The second shot on the par-5 6th hole plays significantly uphill to a blind landing area. Making the shot even more difficult is the fairway, which slopes hard from left to right toward the ocean.

noting where the bottom of your swing is, and place the ball there. As for the swing, take a divot after the ball with your hybrid or fairway wood so you don't catch the top half of the ball. You might still catch it a little thin, but you'll get some distance out of it instead of topping it.

Also, know your limits. Have you ever hit a blind approach shot onto the green from 225 yards out, off a downhill, sidehill lie? Probably not very often. The way to make par on this hole is to choose a club you can hit approximately 165–170 yards, to the top of the hill. (You need to figure in an extra 15 yards for the hill.) A more-lofted club will make topping the ball less likely. If you bombed your drive and must go for the green, make sure you get a good line, commit to it, and swing away with confidence.

## 4. Tee Shot on No. 7

The pros will tell you that you want to make Pebble Beach bleed early and get as much under par as you can through seven holes. After that, you just try to hang on.

The par-3 7th is considered the last of these "easy" holes. But it's one of those "easy-tough" holes for the average golfer, and it can be one of the hardest holes on the course if the wind is really blowing. What makes it challenging, even on the calmest days, is that it always leaves you in-between clubs. The yardage (98 yards from the gold tees) plays significantly downhill, which begs the question: Just how far does it play? Is it a full sand wedge? A three-quarter pitching wedge?

The other thing that comes into play is its history. People want to do well on No. 7 because it's one of the most photographed, picturesque

**While only 98 yards from the gold tees, the par-3 7th hole often leaves you guessing—hard sand wedge or easy pitching wedge?**

holes in all of golf, and they know their friends are going to ask them how they scored on it. For these reasons, a lot of golfers wind up steering or guiding the shot and either pull it into the left greenside bunker or thin it over the green. It's no different than having a straight three-foot putt: it's hard not to look to see where the ball goes, even before it reaches the hole.

To walk away with a three or birdie on No. 7, you must trust what you're thinking. Once you decide it's an 80-yard shot and a full sand wedge, make the very best swing you can and see what happens. Be confident in your decision. The other thing you can do is preplay the shot in your mind (to the desired result) in practice. Going in, you've seen the scorecard, and you know it's going to play as an 80- or 85-yard shot. Well, if you know that, then practice your 80-yard swing on the range before you go out and play. This will remove much of the doubt and fear because you will have already rehearsed the shot beforehand.

## 5. Tee Shot on No. 1

Much like the tee shot on No. 7, I think this one is frightening to most golfers because they attach so much history to the course. Tiger Woods, Jack Nicklaus, Sam Snead, and Arnold Palmer all walked these grounds. All the best players, from Woods, Nicklaus, and Tom Watson to Johnny Miller and Phil Mickelson, have won here. They think it's arguably the best golf course in the world.

**The par-4 1st hole at Pebble Beach attracts a lot of spectators—and butterflies in golfers' stomachs. Make sure to run through your normal pre-shot routine and take several deep breaths before pulling the trigger.**

So when they get up to hit their first tee shot, their hearts are nearly pounding out of their chests. Add in the people milling around the pro shop watching, and it's quite a nerve-wracking experience if you've never been through it.

What they're dealing with is adrenaline that they've built up in their own minds. This adrenaline is going to make them grip the club tighter, swing harder, and do things in a hurried manner. One of the ways to reduce the effects of adrenaline is to take some deep breaths (in through your nose and out through your mouth) as you're hitting your final few putts on the practice green and then walk slowly to the first tee. This will help slow your heart rate down, as well as your movements in general. Take a few more deep breaths on the tee. Keep in mind that these nerves will go away as soon as you hit your tee shot, so picture yourself standing in the fairway with a short iron in your hand or standing on the next tee box.

For more on the first-tee jitters, refer back to Chapter 1.

## 6: Third Shot on No. 18

Most golfers, if they play the hole the way it was designed, will have a short or mid-iron into the green. The key is to place your second shot on the ocean side of the fairway so you're not impeded by the large Monterey cypress tree that guards the right entrance to the green. If your second shot is too far right, you'll have to try to cut the ball around the tree, which requires starting the ball directly at the Pacific Ocean.

**From tee to green, there's always trouble lurking on the 18th hole. The third shot plays uphill into a right-to-left wind, and if you're not careful you could find your ball bounding along the rocks.**

Even if you do approach the green from the left side of the fairway, you still face an imposing third shot that plays slightly uphill into a right-to-left wind, with the ocean on the left and a large frontal bunker covering the right half of the green. The left side of the green also runs toward the ocean, so it appears as if everything is pushing you in that direction.

On any approach shot like this, where there are hazards all around, it's very important that you have a precise yardage into the green. Look to see where the flag is located—is it in the front, center, or back?—and adjust accordingly. Don't just go by the yardage marker in the fairway, because that only gives you the distance to the middle of the green. Look at the trees or flags to see which way the wind is blowing, since that's the approximate height your ball will be traveling in the air. At Pebble Beach, you can look to the two chimneys (or American flags) on top of The Lodge and see which way the smoke is blowing.

Also factor in whether the hole is playing uphill or downhill and the temperature. The 18th plays slightly uphill, and the temperature is usually cool—which means the ball won't travel as far—so you need to add more yardage to make sure you clear the front bunker. If after all this you're still unsure, hit a club that will leave you a little short of the green and chip on.

## 7. Pitch over Greenside Bunker on No. 14

The par-5 14th at Pebble Beach played as the most difficult par-5 on the PGA Tour in 2008,

The raised frontal bunker on the par-5 14th hole hides the severely sloped green behind it and makes the approach shot play 15 yards longer, even from as close as 50 yards.

with a stroke average of 5.3. It also wreaked havoc at the 2010 AT&T Pebble Beach National Pro-Am, when Bryce Molder and Paul Goydos made back-to-back quads (nine strokes) on the hole in the final round. Goydos was leading at the time. It's a three-shot hole for virtually every player; one that forces you to make birdie with your wedges.

What makes this hole so challenging, even for the best players in the world, is that it plays significantly uphill. You've got to advance your second shot long enough to have a reasonable shot at hitting the severely sloped green, which is hidden by a huge frontal bunker. The bunker, because it's raised, is a menacing sight to the average golfer, especially as he gets closer to the green.

At Pebble Beach, you'll be confronted with all types of intimidating pitch shots over bunkers, and No. 14 is no exception. The key is to recognize that it is playing uphill, and it's not flat yardage. If you have 50 yards to the pin and you hit a 50-yard shot, you're going to be in the bunker. It's still a partial swing, but you've got to add about 15 yards to clear the lip and have any chance of two-putting. If you're short or long and left, you've got virtually no chance to get the ball up and down.

If you're not sure of the carry distance, make a rehearsal swing that you know is going to be too long—that is sure to get you there—and one that is too short. Choose the one in the middle and make that your swing. If you're going to make a mistake, do so with a swing that is too long because, more often than not, you're not going to make perfect contact. Besides, it's better to be staring at a chip or pitch for your next shot than the face of a bunker so large you can't see the putting surface.

## 8. Left Greenside Bunker Shot on No. 7

This bunker attracts a lot of balls, and more than a few butterflies, when you're standing over your ball because you look directly at the ocean. Catch the ball just a little thin, and you either hit it into the lip of the bunker or into the ocean. Compounding the difficulty of this shot is that you do have a high lip to navigate and very little green to work with; there's not a lot of room to stop the ball, and in many instances, the ball will run across the green into another bunker. Because it's a high lip, you have to make a big enough swing to get the ball up and out, and that takes courage with the ocean so close.

So just how do you hit this shot hard enough to get it out but soft enough to keep it on the putting surface? First of all, you've got to spend more time practicing from the sand. The reason the pros are so comfortable in sand is because they've spent countless hours honing their greenside bunker skills. You also have to overcome your fear of skulling the ball, which is what everyone dreads on this shot. You do that through practice but also by following a few simple set-up and swing keys. First, make sure to play the ball in the middle of your stance and, most importantly, anchor your weight onto your left (forward) leg at address. Have the feeling that your left shoulder is lower than your right and

The left greenside bunker on the par-3 7th hole is one of the busiest in the world, and can be quite intimidating, too, as you must hit directly toward the ocean.

in line with your left hip. The average golfer tends to fall back onto his trail leg to help the ball up, which is why he skulls it, because the clubhead bottoms out too early and ascends into the ball.

As for the swing, think about throwing a divot of sand onto the green; the ball will ride out on this pillow of sand, in the same direction as the sand. Make a big-enough arm swing (from 10 to 2 o'clock) to displace this pile of sand, because it's not going to move as easily as the ball. Swing to a complete finish. Also make sure your sternum stays centered over the ball through impact, so you don't fall back.

**The 10th fairway slopes hard from left to right, toward the ocean, making it very difficult to control your balance and your ball flight.**

## 9. Downhill, Sidehill Approach Shot on No. 10

Like many of the outward holes at Pebble Beach, the fairway on this par-4 hole slopes hard from left to right, toward the ocean. This slice lie creates a daunting second shot for most golfers, especially when you consider the green is set off to the right and looks as if it's going to fall into the ocean. Any approach shot that veers just a little to the right is headed for the surf.

Whenever you face an awkward lie such as this, balance is the first priority. Settle your weight in the arches of your feet, about an inch forward of your ankle joints. If your weight is in the right place, you should have an easy time lifting and tapping your heels on the ground. Get your shoulders and hips as square, or parallel, to the hill as you can and swing to a balanced finish. (Note: It helps to take more club than necessary—i.e., a 6-iron over a 7—because the severity of the lie won't allow you to hit the ball perfectly, and it helps you to swing more in balance.)

With any hilly lie, the shot tends to move in the direction of the slope, which is from left to right on No. 10. The reason the ball curves to the right is because the club is coming in on a steeper angle, which leads to a fade or a slice (due to an open clubface). For this reason, and because you're bound to be a little tense with the ocean off to the right, you need to borrow more to the left than is necessary. On No. 10, you want to aim at the left greenside bunker and allow the ball to work to the right, toward the center of the green. Make a couple of rehearsal

## Honorable Mention: Most Feared Shots at Pebble Beach

- Tee shot on No. 3
- Left greenside bunker shot on No. 3
- Pitch over left greenside bunker on No. 4
- Second shot on No. 9
- Tee shot on No. 10
- Putt on No. 11 from above the hole
- Tee shot on No. 17 to left pin position
- Second shot on No. 18

swings that are as tension-free as possible, especially on the forward half of the swing. Find your balance points at address and repeat your rehearsal swing. If you can do that and borrow more real estate to the left, you should find yourself nice and dry, maybe even pin high.

## 10. Long Bunker Shot on No. 17

The massive bunker fronting the green on No. 17 attracts about as many balls as the left greenside bunker on No. 7, because it's so big. It stands ready to swallow up any shot that comes up short of the hole. From the very back of the bunker, you have to carry the ball about 35 yards, and once again, if you skull it, you're looking at the possibility of being in the ocean or facing a super-delicate pitch to a very narrow green.

With long bunker shots, there's even a greater propensity to skull the ball or leave it in the sand. Again, just as I discussed earlier for

On long bunker shots, like this one on No. 17, choose your 9-iron or pitching wedge and make your normal 10 to 2 o'clock bunker swing.

the greenside bunker shot on No. 7, you need to put some safety factors in place (weight forward, ball in center of stance, swing from 10 to 2 o'clock, and splash the sand out).

A great drill to practice at your home course or even outside the bunker is to make some swings, removing your right hand off the club shortly after impact. This will keep the club moving through the sand, which is vital if you want to get the ball on the green from 30 yards out.

Because the ball has farther to travel, you need to switch to a less-lofted club, such as a pitching wedge or maybe even a 9- or 8-iron. The farthest anyone should attempt a splash bunker shot is one third of the total distance he hits that same club outside of the bunker. For example, if a full sand wedge for you is 75 yards, the longest bunker shot you should play with a sand wedge is 25 yards—and that's with a *full* swing. For the 35-yard bunker shot on No. 17, you're probably best hitting a pitching wedge or 9-iron with your normal 10 to 2 o'clock bunker swing. The ball will come out lower because of less loft but will stop much sooner than you think, so make your full bunker swing.

More than a few rounds at Pebble Beach have begun to unravel at the par-4 8th hole, the first in a very difficult stretch of four consecutive par-4s.

# Chapter 8

# Bouncing Back

**T**hrough six holes, you're playing lights out! You're thinking to yourself, "Wow, Pebble Beach isn't all that hard." Standing on the tee at the par-3 7th with a sand wedge in your hands, no wind, and only 98 yards between you and the flag, you're staring down a real birdie opportunity and a chance to get your round back to even par.

Even par through seven holes on your first trip around Pebble Beach! You're living the dream.

Then, suddenly, your dream becomes a nightmare. You pull your tee shot into the left greenside bunker, then skull your next shot into the Pacific, not far from where the sea otters are frolicking in the surf. Your fourth shot barely clears the bunker; you chip on, two-putt, and walk away with a quadruple-bogey 7. Ouch! On the next hole, determined to get these strokes back in a hurry, you go for the green on your second shot from 210 yards and hit a thin, dying quail that plunges into the ocean chasm separating the fairway from the green. After another triple bogey, and doubles on Nos. 9 and 10, you're seething and wondering just how all this happened after such a great start.

You have just experienced what is commonly referred to in golf as "having the wheels fall off your game." It happens to even the best of players: John Daly shot an 88 during a PGA TOUR event in 2008, making a 10 on one hole and shooting a back-nine 51; Gil Morgan, the first golfer ever to reach double digits under par in a U.S. Open (he got to 12-under par in the third round of the 1992 U.S. Open at

# Laird's Lessons

## Bouncing Back

**1. Play to Your Personal Par:** Use your handicap to determine a realistic par for each hole; stop trying to play like a scratch golfer.

**2. Use Caution on the Tee:** After a bad hole, play it safe and choose a club on the next tee that will help you get your confidence back.

**3. Learn to Recognize Tension:** Recognize when the environment is stressing you, and plan for how that stress is going to affect your shots.

**4. Don't Attach Yourself to the Outcome:** Forget your negative history with a particular shot; instead, embrace the challenge with a fresh attitude and change the results.

**5. Take a "Second-Shot" Mentality:** Approach your first shot like it's a mulligan, and swing away like you've already put the bad result behind you.

**6. Keep Your Chin Up:** Follow Annika Sorenstam's advice and stop berating yourself after every bad shot. Walk the course with your head held high and it will start to impact your game.

**7. Take the SAT Approach:** Use sports psychologist Dr. Glen Albaugh's postshot process to identify mistakes and reframe them.

Pebble Beach), shot 77-81 on the weekend and finished at 5 over par. Even Tiger Woods shot an 81 in the third round of the 2002 British Open at Muirfield, recording seven bogeys and two double bogeys in his first 14 holes.

Muirfield was an aberration for Woods, whose mental toughness and ability to grind things out is the stuff of legends. No player in the history of golf has grinded out more 69s and 71s when his game was admittedly off than Woods. In this chapter, I'll explain how the best players have a plan so that when the wheels start to come off the wagon, they know how to put them back and pull the cart into the barn. They find a way to bounce back from their very bad holes, and you can, too, by practicing a little more emotional control and patience and understanding what your tendencies are when your game comes under duress.

## 1. Play to Your Personal Par

One way to keep the wheels from flying off is to have realistic expectations going into the round. If you're an 18-handicap playing a difficult course like Pebble Beach for the first time, you can expect to card some bogeys and double bogeys.

Most recreational golfers set par as the gold standard on every hole, even though their handicap suggests a bogey—sometimes even a double bogey—would be a good score for them. It's as if par is the only number that matters. I see more golfers grind on a 6-foot putt for par than they do on a birdie putt of the same length! It's crazy. The fact is, par is a predetermined number of strokes per hole that's designed for a scratch golfer, not an 18-handicap.

**Play to your personal par, not the one on the scorecard. If you were to give yourself an extra stroke per hole at Pebble Beach, your personal par on the par-5 6th hole (pictured here) would be six.**

The handicap system exists for a reason, and that's to help you be more competitive with other golfers and enjoy the game more. The key word there is *enjoy*. You can't play your best golf if you're stressed out before every shot. It goes back to what Johnny Miller said earlier in Chapter 3: you have to look at each shot as being fun.

The next time you play, set a personal par for each hole, one that is more attainable via your skill level. For example, if you're an 18-handicap, add a stroke to each hole so that if you're playing the par-5 6th hole at Pebble Beach, your personal par on that hole is six. Or, if your handicap is

higher, ask yourself what your average score would be on that hole if you played it 10 times and make that your personal par. If you start to improve and find it too easy to attain your personal par, then you can change it. If you take this approach and keep your expectations realistic, you won't find yourself trying to hit the perfect shot into every hole as much, and you'll start to avoid those big numbers that can loosen the bolts on those wheels.

## 2. Use Caution on the Tee

Most golfers, when they come off a double bogey or worse on a hole, will try to get it all back on their next tee shot. What happens? They give it something extra and wind up missing the fairway by some 30 or 40 yards. That's a surefire way to make another double bogey.

The fastest way to lose control of a round is to follow one mistake with another, and the driver gives you the greatest chance of making a mistake. So put it away for a few holes. Throughout his major-championship career, whenever Jack Nicklaus had a bad hole, he made sure to take whatever club he felt was necessary to put the ball in play on the next hole—whether it be a 4-iron or a 3-wood—and he hit that club. Nicklaus was more than happy to make par and build some new momentum from there.

Don't let a blip or two in the middle of your round turn into an avalanche of big scores. More often than not these bad runs can be attributed to poor thinking on tee shots. When you feel your game slipping, or you're a little hot under the collar, choose a club you have the utmost confidence in off the tee and hit that until you get your rhythm and confidence back.

Nothing calms the nerves or fears more than a perfect drive in the middle of the fairway.

## 3. Learn to Recognize Tension

I was recently playing with a friend of mine, and his swing was looking better than I'd ever seen it. It had a nice path and tempo to it, and he appeared to be in total control of his game…until a large hole in the Earth shook him up. His first attempt with a hybrid to clear the ocean chasm on the 8th hole started on line, but it then veered sharply to the right and tumbled toward the cliff below. He then topped his second effort and after two more failed attempts to clear the hazard, decided he'd had enough and trudged onward.

I asked him, "What was different about this shot?" Because up until then, he had been cruising along and swinging with a lot of confidence. He said he didn't know, that "his swing felt the same as it did on all the other holes." I then asked him, "Well, what did the ball

DANGER
STEEP
CLIFF

The environment can create a lot of stress for you on the golf course. If your tendency under pressure is to fade the ball, aim left and play for the curve, as I'm doing here on my approach shot into the par-4 8th hole.

# Jack Nicklaus: How to Avoid the Big Numbers

Jack Nicklaus didn't win 18 major titles by playing carelessly. The Golden Bear managed his game meticulously and, for the most part, stayed away from the costly double and triple bogeys that can sabotage a major championship bid.

"I tried not to make any bogeys or doubles," said Nicklaus, who recorded a remarkable 67 top-10 finishes in majors. "The whole key to winning a major championship is to not have any disastrous holes. I rarely made doubles in majors. When I found myself making doubles, it was because of real stupidity on my part for not really playing the hole the way I should—although sometimes you might get a water hazard, and you can't really avoid it. I'm not going to gamble at making birdie if it means I might make a double or triple bogey. That's a pretty bad gamble. That's how you lose golf tournaments, immediately."

In the rare instances when Nicklaus did make a big number on a hole, it didn't stay with him for long.

**Jack Nicklaus at the Bing Crosby National Pro-Am, playing next to an ocean that is anything but peaceful.** Photo courtesy Getty Images

"There is very little you can do about it," said Nicklaus. "If you are early in the tournament or your round, you say, 'Well, let's don't do that again, and let's don't be stupid. I've given away a couple of strokes, I don't want to give away any more.' I didn't respond by getting more aggressive; I probably was more conservative until I could get my feet back on the ground."

do differently?" And he said, "It curved to the right." I said, "A-ha!"

Whenever you hit shots that are aberrations, that are the opposite of what you've been hitting all day, you know it's the environment that's causing it. The environment stresses you. And what do golfers do when they're under duress? They tend to tense up in their upper body and grip the club a little tighter during the swing, which prevents the clubface from squaring up and leads to the dreaded left-to-right ball. Tension can lead to other types of mistakes, but

more often than not, it's a major cause of slicing the ball.

Had my friend been aware that his tendency under pressure was to fade or slice the ball, he could have planned for it. When we played the same hole a few days later, I had him aim at the glove-shaped bunker about 40 yards short and left of the green, and he hit his approach shot to about 20 feet.

Sam Snead used to say, "Dance with who brung ya." If he showed up in the morning with a fade swing, that's what he'd play with on the course, and then he fixed his swing later on the practice range. Well, if you know you're going to slice it, aim more to the left of your target. Knowing you hit the ball one way, anticipate what it's going to do and play the shot that way.

## 4. Don't Attach Yourself to the Outcome

One of the other causes of tension in the swing is fear—fear of the outcome. Using my friend again as an example, he started talking about all the times he previously hit the ball in the ocean on the eighth hole well before we ever got to the hole. Golfers are like that: they remember all of their bad shots, not the good ones. By conjuring up this bad history, they can't help but think about the outcome before they ever play the shot.

To play tension-free golf, you must be able to close this cycle of negativity and stay focused on the shot at hand. I like to use the acronym NATO,

# Arnold Palmer: Assess Where You Are

If anyone knows something about bouncing back, it's Arnold Palmer. Entering the final round of the 1960 U.S. Open at Cherry Hills trailing by seven shots, Palmer drove the green on the par-4, 346-yard opening hole and stormed back to win his first and only U.S. Open title. Palmer closed with a final-round 65, defeating a young 20-year-old amateur by the name of Jack Nicklaus by two shots.

Palmer's advice to golfers, whether they're trying to bounce back from a bad hole or a tough situation in life, is to "summarize where you are, what your opportunities are for recovery, and go for it."

Palmer did just that prior to teeing off in the final round at Cherry Hills. Assessing the situation, he told Pittsburgh sports writer Bob Drum that a 65 would give him an even-par total of 280 and a good shot at winning the championship. Then he went out and did it.

The same approach is needed when you're coming off a costly double bogey or worse.

"Of course, when you do that, your frame of mind is always bad, and the first thing you want to do is get a birdie to make up for your mistakes," said Palmer. "But sometimes that causes you more trouble. Sometimes we lose strokes, and then we get excited, and it costs us more strokes. You have to give that some consideration after a bad hole. I wouldn't get too conservative, but on the other hand, I'd be sure not to lose more strokes to aggressive play."

Palmer didn't try to make up all seven strokes in a hurry at Cherry Hills; he stuck with his game plan, which was to drive the green on No. 1 and get to even par for the tourney. Many times, amateurs have a good round going and start looking ahead or counting strokes. They're standing on the seventh tee at Pebble, and they're already thinking ahead to the tough stretch of par-4 holes coming up or the monstrous par-5 14th. They're thinking, "Well, if I could just get through holes 8, 9, and 10 at even or 1 over par, I'm in good shape." Such thinking can be dangerous, said Palmer, and unwise.

"One of the things I've always done is take counsel of where I am and what I've done," said Palmer. "Then I refer to the basics of everything I know and what I know best—whether it be in golf or life—and give it my absolute best shot. Don't be too anxious to do something dramatic. Be sure what you know and what you want to do with those shots."

or *Not Attached To Outcome*, to describe this mind-set. Remember, you're playing a game, and the definition of *play* is to have fun. If it so happens that you have a poor history with a particular shot, well, great, you've got another opportunity to beat it. Embrace the challenge. That's a much better attitude than thinking, "Oh, here we go, I've got this darn shot again."

Are you going to face the shot with feelings of doom and gloom, like the *Winnie the Pooh* character Eeyore, or are you going to be the more upbeat Tigger and think, "Oh yippee, I've got a chance to do this again! I know I can get there with my second shot."

Change your attitude, and you'll change your results.

## 5. Take a "Second-Shot" Mentality

How many times have you hit a bad shot, only to drop a second ball and then, without even pausing to give it a thought, knocked your next shot stiff? Or maybe you hit your tee shot out of bounds, and after reteeing it, you smacked the next drive down the center of the fairway? It happens all the time, right? And it tends to drive you mad because you're left wondering why you didn't hit your first ball like that.

The reason this happens so frequently is because, with the second shot, there's nothing attached to the outcome. You figure, "What else could go wrong?" So you step up there without any hesitation or fear that you could hit it out of

**Arnold Palmer occasionally found himself in tough spots at Pebble Beach, such as in 1964 when he found himself on the rocks at the 17th hole.** Ted Durien Collection

bounds, and you nut it! You hit the perfect shot. The experience of that also shows you can do it, which will give you more confidence down the road.

If this works so well, then why not take this second-shot mentality with you out on the course when things are not going so well? As you stand over the ball, take the approach in your mind that you've already experienced the bad result and swing away. With this second-shot mentality applied to your first ball, you'll be free to swing without any fear of consequences. You'll make a tension-free swing, and the ball will just get in the way of that action. Try it the next time you encounter a tough stretch of holes. Take a mulligan on your first ball and see if that tricks your mind enough to get you to swing away with confidence and good rhythm and timing.

## 6. Keep Your Chin Up

There were 14 teenagers in the field at the 2003 U.S. Women's Open at Pumpkin Ridge,

Keep your chin up, no matter how poorly you might be playing. This projects a positive vibe and gives you a better chance of turning things around.

including one famous 13-year-old, Michelle Wie, and one not-so-famous 13-year-old, Sydney Burlison. Sydney, an eighth grader from nearby Salinas, California, was a student of mine at the time and a darn good player. She was medalist at the Daly City, California, qualifier for the Women's Open.

This particular Open happened to come just weeks after Annika Sorenstam captured the world's curiosity by playing in the PGA TOUR's Bank of America Colonial tournament in Fort Worth, Texas. While on the range at Pumpkin Ridge, I happened to bump into Annika's former Swedish National Team coach and mentor Pia Nilsson, and I asked her what Annika's preparation was for the week. She said Annika was working hard and that she was "ready to win." I then asked her if she could share anything with young Sydney that might help her cope with the pressure of playing on such a big stage. She told us how Annika's one and only goal for the first round was to walk with her chin up. No matter what happened on the course, she was going to keep her chin up, her shoulders back, and walk like a champion golfer.

I thought this was great advice, not just for Sydney but for every golfer. Think about it: When you're sulking on the course or berating yourself for hitting a bad shot, what do you do? You tend to walk around with your shoulders slumped and your head down. You assume a very negative body language, and that reflects in your performance. By keeping your chin up and walking like a matador, you not only give off a more positive vibe, but you're able to take in

## Tom Watson: Monitor Your Grip Pressure

Tom Watson was leading the Bing Crosby National Pro-Am in the final round one year when he ran into trouble on the 8th hole, the first of four very difficult par-4s in a row at Pebble Beach.

"I pulled it left off the tee, then I tried to go for the green, and I hit it in the hazard," recalls Watson. "I think I wound up making an [quadruple bogey] eight. It was all downhill from there. If you've lost your sense of feel and confidence, Pebble Beach is not the place to get it back. I did not respond well. Normally, if I have a bad hole, I'll respond like a cornered animal—I'll respond quickly and precisely. That eight ruined my day."

Watson says that on many occasions, a bad hole or series of bad holes can be traced to grip pressure.

"When things are going badly, you tend to grip tighter on the club, and your rhythm in your swing is thrown off because of that," says Watson. "Any time you have a bad stretch of holes after a good start, no matter where it is, you try to readjust and make sure you have the same grip pressure you had earlier in the round. That's something I tell all amateurs, that grip pressure is probably an afterthought when things are going badly."

One way to loosen your death grip on the club and get a feel for the proper grip pressure is to turn the club upside down so you're holding it by the clubhead and swinging the handle.

"That's a great lesson for amateurs or anybody," said Watson. "I've seen some pros use that on Tour. You get a feel for the clubhead back, and you get your hands involved with the clubhead. You'll lose that feel if you grip on too tightly."

the surrounding landscape, breathe in the fresh air, and keep your emotions more in check.

As a reminder to my young students to keep their chins up, I give them a tongue compressor with the word *attitude* written on it. I have them rest the stick between their chin and collarbone, which gives them a good visual and a feel for what it's like to push your chin up. (At home, you can do this by making a letter *L* with your thumb and forefinger and placing that between your collarbone and chin.)

When you're out on the course, magic can strike at any time. You can chop up a hole and then drain a 50-footer or chip in and still make your par. But you can only be ready for this magic to happen if your attitude is good. It's very easy to get ticked off if things are going badly, but the harder thing to do is keep a positive attitude. That's the mark of a great champion like Annika. When things aren't going right, can you keep your chin up and remain upbeat?

I see people playing Pebble Beach for the first time, cussing and slamming their clubs down on the ground. I think, *Why?* I mean, where else would you rather be? Back in the office working? Keep your chin up, take in the beauty of the landscape, and enjoy the camaraderie with your friends. This type of attitude not only makes the game more fun, but it allows you to play much better.

## 7. Take the SAT Approach

As I discussed earlier in this chapter, most golfers only recall their bad shots, not the good ones. However, the game's best players only remember the good ones. When they hit a shot they like, you see them staring it down, soaking in the feeling of a well-struck ball. If they do happen to hit a poor shot, you rarely see them pouting about it. Yes, they might visibly display some anger for a second or two, but then it's gone. They replace it with a rehearsal swing or two, reframing the shot in their mind the way they intended it to come out.

This is all part of their postshot routine. Yes, I know what you're thinking: "I'm still trying to develop a consistent preshot routine." But you want to soak in the good shots and also analyze the bad ones, so you can fix them. If you hit a bad shot, try to determine what the cause of it was. Was it the environment? Was it the fear of hitting the ball into the water? Was it something mechanical in your swing? Was your adrenaline too high and, if so, how can you change that the next time around?

A friend of mine, sports psychologist Dr. Glen Albaugh, uses the acronym SAT (*S*trategy, *A*im, and *T*rust) to guide his golfers through the postshot routine process. He has them ask a series of three questions: 1) How was your strategy on the shot? Perhaps it wasn't your execution but the fault of the previous shot because it left you with such a horrible lie. 2) How was your aim? You hit the ball really solidly, but it went out of bounds. So how did it get there? Were you aiming in that direction? 3) Did you trust what you were doing? You were between clubs and chose a 7-iron, but when you got up to the ball, it didn't look right to you. Still, you went ahead and hit the shot anyway and pushed it into the very greenside bunker you were trying to avoid in the first place. In this case, it wasn't the swing but a lack of trust.

The benefit to using the SAT system is that it allows you to identify your mistakes and reframe them: "It was a really good swing. I just didn't trust the club I chose, so next time I'm going to go with my instincts, grip down more, and let it go." You work on your postshot routine, as well as your preshot routine, and you'll learn to trust your decisions more and keep those wheels firmly on the ground.

**Analyze your bad shots so you're less likely to repeat them in the future. Ask yourself: How was my strategy? My aim? Did I follow through with my intention? By working in a postshot routine, you'll learn to make better decisions and keep your bad shots to a minimum.**

# Tom Kite's Keys to Handling Adversity

During the final round of the 1992 U.S. Open at Pebble Beach, wind blew the wheels off many a player's wagon, leaving debris strewn all over the course. Only five players broke par, and 20 failed to break 80. It was so bad that when Colin Montgomerie finished early in the afternoon at even par—with many golfers still out on the course—Jack Nicklaus congratulated him for winning the U.S. Open.

Someone forgot to tell Tom Kite, however. Kite, playing in the final group that day, faced the harshest of conditions (40-mph wind gusts) but was still able to hold it together, shooting an even-par 72 to beat Jeff Sluman by two strokes and win his first major. Some people say it was the greatest round ever played in a major championship.

"It was a tremendous advantage for me having grown up in Texas, because I encountered so many difficult conditions there—hard, dry fairways, floods, high winds, heat, Bermuda grass greens," said Kite. "I'm a big believer in playing a lot of golf under different circumstances on different golf courses. Don't play your course all the time, over and over and over to where it's just automatic. Go play some different courses. Go play in different conditions and go play in some tournaments. That's when you find out how to handle the nervousness and emotions."

While many of the players folded on that Sunday, Kite flourished. One of the reasons why was his ability to stay in the present and not look back or think too far ahead. The latter is easy to do when you're playing for a major championship or on pace to shoot a career-best round. The former is easy to do when you're coming off a bad hole or series of holes or a missed short putt that cost you a par or birdie.

"The biggest trick is to keep reminding yourself that you can't control the past or the future; you can only control what's going on right now," said Kite. "When the wheels have come off, the word *have* is in the past tense, so you need to get out of the past tense and quit thinking about what has already occurred. The better job you can do staying in the present tense, the better off you are. The future will get there soon enough."

Kite says that his caddie on the Champions Tour, Sandy Jones, does a good job of keeping him in the present.

"She's always reminding me that it's all about this shot," Kite said. "If I hit a bad drive, she reminds me on the next shot to pick a target. Basically, she's saying, 'Focus in on what you're doing right now. You're not playing that last hole right now.'"

One other thing Kite does immediately following a particularly poor drive or shot is reframe it so the shot comes out the way he intended it to. That makes the poor outcome easier to forget.

"Whether I physically make another practice swing or do it in my mind, I always play the shot well," said Kite. "I'll do that even with my good shots. If you hit a great shot, there's no reason not to improve upon that. Feel the tempo, rhythm, and balance that allows you to hit that shot again. Certainly, if you hit a poor shot, you don't want to carry that on from shot to shot. Gary Player and Tom Watson are notorious about this. If they hit a bad shot, they go over and make a practice swing to try to get the feeling for exactly what they want to accomplish."

**Tom Kite escaping from a bunker on the par-3 17th hole at Pebble Beach during the final round of the 1992 U.S. Open.** PBC Archives

New bunkers on the short par-4
3rd hole penalize those golfers
who hit through the fairway.

# Chapter 9

# How to Major in Architecture

**S**ince opening in 1919, Pebble Beach Golf Links has undergone some significant tweaks, but the original design of Jack Neville and Douglas Grant still retains its natural splendor and rugged coastline features.

The most recent enhancements came under the watchful eye of Arnold Palmer, whose design company added length and grit to the course in preparation for the 2010 U.S. Open, the fifth held at Pebble Beach—1972, '82, '92, and 2000 were the others. Several greens and bunkers were rebuilt or installed, including three new fairway bunkers along the right side of the $3^{rd}$ fairway (photo, left) and five new bunkers on the left side of the sixth fairway.

The biggest change was to the length of the course. Three new championship tees were added to the par-4 $9^{th}$, $10^{th}$, and $13^{th}$ holes, stretching them by more than 150 yards combined. A new tee box was also added on No. 11. At 7,040 yards, the 2010 U.S. Open will play almost 200 yards longer than it did in 2000 (6,846 yards).

Why make Pebble Beach more challenging? After all, the only player to finish under par in 2000 was Tiger Woods. The changes were made to bring the course more in line with today's major-championship venues. (Bethpage Black, host of the 2009 U.S. Open, played at more than 7,400 yards.) By lengthening several of the holes, players will now have to hit longer clubs into the course's smallish greens. No longer will players be able to drive the ball to the bottom of the hill and fire a short wedge into the

# How to Major in Architecture

**1. Recognize the Misdirection Play:** Course architects change things up from hole to hole to keep you from getting too comfortable and to challenge all facets of your game. Be ready by practicing many different types of shots from various lies.

**2. Which Way Do I Go?:** Don't get fooled by the angling of tee boxes, because many are designed to push your ball out of play. Find a nearby target that helps you to align properly.

**3. Bunkers—The Art of Deception:** More than 100 bunkers at Pebble Beach effectively tighten both fairways and greens, but they also are designed to deceive golfers. These tips will help you see the bunkers for what they are and use them as a clue for selecting the right club and target.

**4. Par-4s vs. Par-5s:** Learn the critical design differences between these types of holes, and why they demand contrasting strategic approaches. If you start thinking like an architect while negotiating a hole—identifying its defense mechanisms and the risks inherent in every shot—you'll start seeing better results on your scorecard.

green, as they once were able to on the par-4 9th. The driving areas will be more challenging, too, because players will have to hit their tee shots into the neck—or skinniest part—of each fairway to have a short club into the green.

Players will have to shape their shots—mostly from right to left—into the slopes if they want to keep the ball in the fairway.

Because of better equipment, players are spinning the ball less today and hitting the ball straighter. The United States Golf Association is hoping that Palmer's adjustments will add an element of shotmaking to this year's U.S. Open that has been diminishing from the game the last few years.

The officials at the USGA aren't the only people interested in protecting par; the reason behind just about every course redesign or reshaping today is to enhance the challenge of the game. The architect is the protector of par, and he's going to make you work very hard for yours. If you're not aware of what the architect is trying to do, you will find bogeys much easier to come by than pars.

The following lessons will show how to make more pars by understanding the little nuances and tricks of the architect's trade.

## 1. Recognize the Misdirection Play

Unless he has overpowering stuff, a good baseball pitcher will rarely fire three fastballs in a row to a hitter. The golf course architect thinks the same way: he's not going to follow one dogleg par-4 with another of the same length. He's going to mix things up and force you to hit different shots.

The architects at Pebble Beach throw you a variety of fastballs, sinkers, and change-ups right from the start. On the first two holes, the fairways slope from left to right (slice fairways), but on the 3rd hole, the fairway slides from right to left (hook fairway). The par-4 hole plays downhill, whereas No. 4 plays uphill and No. 5 slightly downhill. The par-5 6th hole plays straight downhill off the tee but then climbs about three or four stories on the second shot, so much so that you can't see the upper fairway or green. The short par-3 7th plays straight downhill, followed by an uphill tee shot on No. 8 and a downhill second shot.

You get the picture by now. The architects are changing gears on you because they want to challenge all facets of your game. Take the 6th hole as an example. The first shot plays significantly downhill from an elevated tee, which gives you the confidence that you can launch the ball to Hawaii. But on the second shot, the situation is reversed: you have a downhill shot that you're trying to hit up this steep hill directly in front of you, and the fairway slopes hard from left to right. Now, you feel like you have to help the ball up in the air, which often leads to a topped shot because the tendency is to lift up through the strike. Add in the slice fairway, and it's not unusual to see many second shots wind up in the ocean off to the right.

The architects are throwing some misdirection at you because they don't want you to get too comfortable out there. If you want to make birdie or par on the 6th hole, then you're going to have to put some trust into a low-lofted club on that second shot. Can you hit it solidly enough to carry the hill and put it on the flat section up top or maybe even reach the green?

Whenever you play a new course for the first time, you must anticipate that the architect is going to switch things up on you and that on one hole the ball might be above your feet on the second shot and on the very next hole it may be below your feet. It might only be a subtle difference, but it's enough to curve the ball or change the trajectory of the shot. If you're ready for that curveball the designer might throw at you, and you practice hitting from all different types of lies, then you will have an easier time making pars.

# Arnold Palmer: Tree Trouble No More

In addition to the new fairway bunkers, several trees have been planted or replaced since the 2000 U.S. Open to help squeeze the landing areas at Pebble Beach. One such tree is a large cypress on the right side of the 14th fairway, about 100 yards from the green on the par-5.

Years ago, a large pine tree overhung the fairway like a huge canopy, almost in the exact same spot. Trailing Jack Nicklaus by one shot in the final round of the 1967 Bing Crosby National Pro-Am, Arnold Palmer attempted to go for the green in two but wound up hitting the top of the tree and losing the ball out of bounds. The unfortunate carom cost him a chance at winning the tournament. The next morning, as he and his wife Winnie were leaving the course, they noticed that the very same tree was lying in the middle of the fairway. A storm had blown through the night before—uprooting it—although many people believe it was Arnie's shot that knocked the tree down.

## 2. Which Way Do I Go?

Another form of misdirection that some architects use is the angling of the tee boxes. Sometimes, they'll stagger them to point you in a direction other than the centerline of the fairway. The back and gold tees on the par-4 15th hole at Pebble, for example, point you directly toward the cart path and the road bordering the right side of the fairway, which is out of bounds. The wind usually blows over your right shoulder, too, which encourages you to hit your tee shot even farther right.

Jack Nicklaus, a natural fader of the ball, used to hit 3-wood on this hole because he found it easier to curve the ball from right to left with it, which is what this tee shot calls for. He hit a position club that he knew he could keep in play. The other thing you can do on this hole is find something to aim your body toward that will point you more to the left, or center, of the fairway. The closer this intermediate target is to you, the better, because it's much easier to aim at something that's near you and not so far away. On this particular hole, you're in luck, because the lines on the edge of the white tee box both point more to the left. Use these lines as your alignment aid, and you should have an easier time avoiding the dreaded left-to-right ball.

**Some tee boxes on the par-4 15th hole point you out of bounds (inset photo, right). Many architects use this angling technique, so be careful. In this instance, you want to align yourself to the lines on the white tee box (main photo), which point slightly left at the fairway below.**

## 3. Bunkers: The Art of Deception

Upon playing Pebble Beach, 1921 U.S. Open champion Jim Barnes said, "It's too dom beautiful; I ken not keep my mind on the game."

Many legends of the game—and those people lucky enough to have played the course—have echoed the same sentiments about Pebble Beach over the years. The stunning ocean vistas, vibrant colors, cypress trees, wildlife,

The kidney-shaped bunker on the par-4 3rd hole (inset) hides much of the fairway, giving off the appearance that there's not much room to fit your tee shot. It also makes the carry seem much longer. Should you opt to cut the corner of the dogleg, make sure you know how far it is to carry the corner and how much curve, or draw, your shot needs.

The smaller bunker to the left of the 5th hole appears to be near the back of the green, but is actually in the middle (inset, opposite). If you bail out to the left and you don't put enough spin on your tee shot, you could very well find this bunker.

and crashing waves all serve as distractions—albeit pleasant ones—as you make your way around the course.

There are many other distractions in place, too, strategically set throughout the course by the architects to intimidate, challenge, and also deceive the golfer. Chief among these man-made distractions are bunkers: Pebble Beach Golf Links has more than 100 of them in all different sizes, depths, and shapes. They don't have names to them, like the Church Pews at Oakmont or the Road Bunker at the Old Course at St. Andrews, but they are unforgettable to those who play Pebble Beach. The left greenside bunker on the par-3 7th hole, for example, is quite possibly the busiest bunker in the world, while the deep bunkered gully short and left of the 9th green makes the ocean seem like a more inviting place to be. Then there's the

# Bobby Clampett: A Splash Here, a Splash There

On the first hole, you get a clear indication as to how most of the greens at Pebble Beach break, which is toward the ocean. But from the fairway, it looks as if the green is tilted from right to left, away from the ocean. This is yet another example of how bunkering can deceive you.

"The bunkers are very tight to the greens, and because of that, you get a lot of buildup on the lips of the bunkers from the splash of the sand," said CBS commentator, teaching professional, and former PGA TOUR player Bobby Clampett, who was born in nearby Monterey, California, and used to sneak onto Pebble Beach regularly before there were rangers. "The sand also gets on the greens and builds them up over time, so they're very high on the edges. I can remember back in high school, the 7th green was incredibly difficult. It was so high on the edges that anything you hit on the edge of the green just bounced forever. You had to lay the ball into the middle of the green, otherwise you weren't going to control the distance of the shot."

The 7th green has lost some of its bite over the years, but as evidenced by the first green, you still have to pay attention to the edges of the greens around Pebble Beach.

"Almost every bunker shot seems to be going downhill because of the splashing of the sand over the years, which makes the penalty for missing the green more severe, especially when the greens get hard and fast," said Clampett.

Clampett is also a course designer whose work includes the recently completed Payne Stewart Golf Club in Branson, Missouri. Clampett, who finished tied for third at the 1982 U.S. Open at Pebble Beach, said he likes to put design features in his courses that remind him of Pebble Beach.

"I was in awe of Pebble Beach when I first stepped on it, and I'm still in awe of it," said Clampett. "To me, it represents everything great about golf."

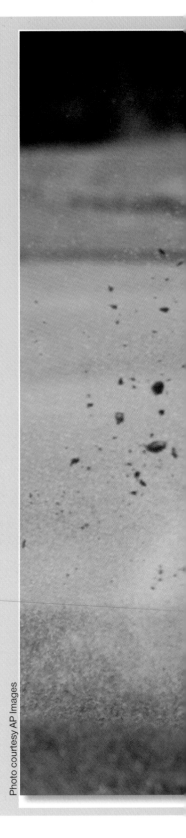

Photo courtesy AP Images

**That's what all of the bunkers at Pebble Beach do: they distract and test you to see if you have the confidence to hit a particular shot. However, they also serve as directional cues and yardage markers, so use them to your advantage as well.**

huge frontal bunker on No. 14, one of those intimidating, to-be-avoided-at-all-costs bunkers.

The primary design function of the bunkers at Pebble Beach is to tighten the fairways and greens so that they create a greater shot value on your drives and approach shots. Among the adjustments Arnold Palmer made to the course for the 2010 U.S. Open was to move the fairway pot bunker on No. 4 15 yards to the right, toward the coastline, and stretch the giant snake-shaped fairway bunker on the left to pinch in the landing area 60 to 100 yards from the green. He also installed a cluster of new bunkers on the left side of the fairway, near the landing area, on No. 6. What this does, besides shrink your landing area, is force you to challenge the right side of the fairway and hit a

draw because the fairway slopes hard from left to right, toward the ocean. Before, you could hit your tee shot directly at the bunker and fade the ball into the fairway, but now you must either hit it dead straight or draw the ball to keep it in play. If you hit into these bunkers, it's very difficult to get the ball to the top of the hill.

One other thing the bunkers do at Pebble Beach is deceive you. The tee shot on the short, dogleg par-4 3rd hole is a perfect example of this. There are two bunkers directly on your line to the fairway, just to the right of the tall cluster of trees you must navigate at the corner of the dogleg. The second, kidney-shaped bunker has been raised considerably to hide the fairway and give off the appearance that there isn't much room to fit your ball into. By taking some of the fairway away visually, it also makes the landing area appear much farther away than it actually is. From the regular (white) tees, it's 165 yards to carry the kidney bunker, but standing over the ball, you'd think it was at least 200 yards. Fortunately, there are markers on the tee telling you how far you have to hit your drive to clear the bunker. The bad news is they've installed three new fairway bunkers on the other side of the fairway to intercept any straight ball, so you either have to draw the ball around the corner or fit your tee shot between the kidney bunker and the new fairway bunkers.

The par-3 5th hole is an even better example of how bunkering can be used to deceive you. The hole, redesigned by Jack Nicklaus in 1998, plays slightly downhill toward the ocean, whereas the previous version used to run inland and uphill. It's home to the second-largest green on the course, although standing on the tee you'd swear it was the smallest. That's because most of the green is hidden from you visually by the large greenside bunker on the right. There's also a second, much smaller trap to the left of the green, which looks to be toward the back of the green but is actually in the middle. From the tee, the obvious play appears to be to aim at the left side of the green, but if you carry it in there with little spin, the ball kicks forward into the bunker, leaving you with a delicate downhill bunker shot to a green that's sloping away from you, toward the ocean.

What you have to realize is that the bunkers are directional cues. The greenside bunker on the right is going to point you to the bunker on the left, but do you know how far it is to this bunker? Sure, it looks farther away, but one look at the yardage book will tell you that it's 142 yards (from the gold tees) to the middle of the green, which is the approximate yardage to the bunker. If it's 120 yards to the front of the green, then ask yourself what club it is you hit 125 to 130 yards; that should put you safely on the green.

The tee shot on No. 5 is the second shortest at Pebble Beach but also one of the most challenging because of the deception created by the bunkers. You have an offensive club (8- or 9-iron) into this green, but can you remain aggressive because the architect is trying to take that mentality away from you visually? That's what all of the bunkers at Pebble Beach do: they distract and test you to see if you have the confidence to hit a particular shot. However, they also serve as directional cues and yardage markers, so use them to your advantage as well.

## 4. Par-4s vs. Par-5s

To understand the differences between most par-4s and par-5s, one doesn't have to look beyond the first two holes at Pebble Beach. The first hole is a relatively short par-4 (346 yards from the gold tees), but it demands you curve the ball from right to left off the tee to keep the ball in the short grass because the fairway slopes from left to right. If you fade your ball, it's going to bounce to the right and miss the fairway. Like many par-4s, the landing area gets significantly narrower as you get closer to the green, like the neck of a wine bottle. The architect is telling you to take the shorter club off the tee and hit to the widest part of the fairway, which on No. 1 is about 150 yards from the center of the green. Should you dare to hit driver around the corner, you'll need to fit your tee shot into the narrowest part of the fairway if you want a crack at birdie; hit your tee shot just a little bit off-line, however, and you're likely to be punching out from behind some trees.

This is the typical blueprint for most par-4s: the architect is going to force you to hit a good tee shot. Should you find the short grass, you'll have a reasonable second shot into the green, open enough to where you'll have many different options. However, should you miss the fairway, you're going to have a challenging second shot out of the rough or out from behind a tree and an even more difficult time making your par.

The par-5s tend to be a little more generous off the tee and then get progressively more challenging as you get closer to the hole. Take the second hole at Pebble Beach, for example: as par-5s go, it's not very long (487 yards from the gold tees). So what do the architects do to increase the difficulty of this hole? First, they pinch the landing area by placing two large bunkers 210 yards from the hole, on either side of the fairway. Should you find the fairway, you must play your second shot from a slice (left to right) fairway lie, with the ball below your feet. Making the second shot even more difficult is a cluster of trees and a large, deep cross-bunker that cuts across the fairway about 75 yards short of the green. Golfers who draw a bad lie off the tee or face a long second shot must decide whether to try and carry the cross-bunker or lay up short of it.

If you're able to clear the cross-bunker but can't get home in two, you've got a very difficult pitch shot to a tiny green well protected by bunkers. It's hard to generate any spin with a partial swing so close to the green. You're better off laying up and hitting a full pitching wedge or 9-iron into the green, although you still have to be very precise with your third shot.

On most par-5s the architect will tempt you to go for the green in two, but he'll make you pay if you hit a poor shot. This is the case on all of the par-5s at Pebble Beach: there's out of bounds to the right on No. 2, in addition to the cross-bunker; there's ocean to the right on No. 6; out of bounds to the left and right on No. 14; and out of bounds right and ocean left on No. 18. The greens on these par-5s are devilishly small, well-bunkered, and anything but flat. This is a defense mechanism a lot of architects will put into place on a par-5 hole because they don't want to make it too easy to hit the green with a short iron—i.e., your third shot. If you play it as a three-shot hole, they want to force you to hit a precise yardage into the green. Keep these things in mind the next time you challenge a par-5, whether you're playing it as a two- or three-shot hole, and you should start seeing better results.

**Most architects will tempt you to go for the green in two on par-5s, but not without great risk, as evidenced here on the par-5 6th hole. Not only must you play to a blind fairway, but you must also contend with a severe sidehill lie that slopes toward the ocean on the right.**

**More shots are wasted around the green than anywhere else, which is why you should spend the majority of your practice time working on your short game.**

# Chapter 10

# How to Get Better

**A**ccording to a recent National Golf Foundation participation study, there were 28.6 million golfers in the United States in 2008. Of these nearly 30 million golfers, only half were able to shoot 100 on a consistent basis; one in four could break 90 consistently.

What does this tell us about the state of the game today? It says that there is *a lot* of room for improvement, from everyone.

The most frequently asked question I hear from golfers is, "How do I get better?" Very rarely, if ever, do I come across a golfer who is satisfied with his or her game—at any point in time—and doesn't think he or she can get better. Even the best players in the world are always striving to improve. Just look at Tiger Woods: What did he do after winning four consecutive majors in 2000 and 2001? He went about changing his swing…for a second time!

How do you get better? You start by making an assessment of your game and everything that impacts it. I like to refer my students to the Circle of Performance model used by my friend Dr. Glen Albaugh, a noted sports psychologist who works with many professional golfers. What the Circle of Performance does is take a holistic approach to your game. You're not going to shoot lower scores by working on swing technique alone; you have to improve the overall quality of your life and game, from better nutrition and health to better course management skills, self-talk (i.e., the inner game), equipment, and family relationships.

At the center, or hub, of this Circle of Performance is the love you have for the game—an unspoken connection you have with the sport and the courses you play. Each aspect of the game I mentioned above acts

# How to Get Better

**1. Start with the Little Victories:** Follow the lead of Seattle Seahawks coach Pete Carroll and find one aspect of your game to improve. When you succeed, this "win" can motivate you in other areas.

**2. Take Inventory of Your Game:** Take a physical analysis of your game to determine where you are wasting the most shots. Once these weak spots have been identified, you can work to fix them—and improve your scores.

**3. Short-Game Practice Drills:** More than half of all shots occur inside 50 yards of the green. Use these drills to improve your short game and save lots of strokes.

**4. Full-Swing Practice Drills:** Put away your driver and make practice time for other clubs that get more use on the course. Five full-swing drills are described that will help improve your game.

**5. Stretch Your Body:** Often, your body's physical limitations, not your swing, prevent you from improving. This stretching regimen will help prepare your muscles for top performance on the course.

**6. Fuel Your Body:** Drinking plenty of water and eating healthy foods on the course are essential for performing at your peak level for a full 18 holes.

**7. Survey Your Equipment:** Make sure that your bag is stocked with the right tools for success. Consider these tips on set makeup, grips, balls, and more.

like a spoke in a wheel, radiating outward from this hub; what you need to do is strike a balance between these spokes if you are to become the 80- or 90-shooter you always aspired to be.

In this chapter, I will touch on a few of these areas that I think are essential to improving your performance on the course. If you work on these drills, fundamentals, and practices over the next few months, you will get better.

## 1. Start with the Little Victories

Before I get into any specific drills or practice plans, remember that there is no miracle diet pill in golf. If you're having a hard time breaking 90, you're not going to become an 80-shooter overnight, no matter how hard you practice. You get better incrementally, by winning the little battles on the course that might seem small in the big picture but eventually add up and make the difference in the long run.

An acquaintance of mine is Pete Carroll, the head coach of the Seattle Seahawks. When Pete was hired by USC in December 2000, he took over a declining program that was coming off three disappointing, mediocre seasons. The Trojans' turnover ratio was one of the worst in the country, so Pete made it a point to address the team's ball security woes from the outset. His mantra his first season was "everything is about the ball." The goal was to not turn the ball over, and after a slow 2–5 start, his teams took 67 of their next 74 games, winning 34 consecutive games at one point and two national championships.

It all started with one win for Carroll and USC, which was to win the turnover battle every game. Most golfers think of winning in terms of the number they shoot on the scorecard, which only impedes their progress. They may play a good round of golf and accomplish several firsts, but if they don't break 80 or shoot their target score, they consider their round a failure. These failures add up over time, not only making the game less enjoyable, but creating a negative, stressful environment that is not conducive to learning and getting better.

Every golfer must define what a win means. It might be as simple as getting past your nerves and hitting the first tee shot at Pebble Beach in play, getting the ball out of the bunker in one shot, or following up one good shot with another for several holes. Maybe it's hitting a draw around the corner on the dogleg-left 3rd hole at Pebble Beach, when you so often slice the ball on that hole. These are all little wins, but by accumulating these victories over time, you'll stay motivated and will want to continue to get better and practice.

## 2. Take Inventory of Your Game

A couple of Novembers ago I was playing a practice round with PGA TOUR player Jason Gore prior to the Callaway Golf Pebble Beach Invitational. Just several months earlier, Gore was a surprise co-leader through 36 holes at the U.S. Open (at Pinehurst), and he had enjoyed a breakthrough season of sorts. I asked him what he was working on in his game at the time, and he said, "You know, I played a lot of rounds with Tiger this year, and I

**If you're going to get serious about improving, start by taking a physical analysis of your game. Learn where you're wasting the most shots.**

realized that Tiger left himself easy putts for par whenever he missed a green. I left myself too many six-footers that I didn't convert."

The great Byron Nelson said a similar thing after his record-setting 1945 season in which he won 11 consecutive tournaments and 18 overall. A reporter asked Nelson why he thought he had such a dominant year, and Lord Byron explained that upon looking at his stats from the previous year, he realized he missed way too many short putts. Then Nelson said that upon further reflection, he realized he wasn't chipping the ball close enough to the hole. He spent the entire off-season working on his chipping. One other thing he did was commit himself to not hitting a careless shot all year. You'll frequently hear Tiger and other players talk about how they're going to play to a conservative target. What they're really saying is that they're not going to hit a careless shot.

If you're going to get serious about improving, start by taking a physical analysis of your game. Learn where you're wasting the most shots. You can do this by tracking such things as fairways hit, greens hit in regulation, putts per round, percentage of three-putts from 30 feet or more, number of greens hit from inside 50 yards, average distance away from the hole on shots inside 50 yards (what I like to refer to as the "red zone"), percentage of up and downs when pitching, chipping, or hitting from the bunker, distance away from the hole on approach shots of 100–150 yards and 150–200 yards, and more. This will give you a snapshot of what you're doing on the course and help you to identify those weaknesses that may not be so obvious at first. Nelson's story is a perfect example of this: at first he thought his short putting was the cause of his troubles on the green, when, in actuality, it was his chipping.

Once you've identified where these weaknesses are, then you can work to fix them, just as Nelson did. If you know, for example, that you're successful getting up and down just 5 percent of the time from the greenside bunker, but you hit 70 percent of your fairways, you can adjust your practice time so you spend 20 minutes in the bunker and five to 10 on the range. That's how golf's best do it: they take inventory of their games at the end of each season and work hard that off-season to correct their faults so they know they won't be an issue the following season.

## 3. Short-Game Practice Drills

To help my students pinpoint their strengths and weaknesses, I encourage them to use a subscription-based Web service called ShotByShot.com, which allows them to print out a downloadable scorecard and track,

among other things, how close they hit their short-game shots (inside 50 yards) to the hole and their percentage of error (greens missed) on these shots. I mention these two statistics because most golfers, while they spend the majority of their practice time on driving and full-swing shots, waste more shots around the green than anywhere else. This should come as no surprise considering more than half of all shots occur inside 50 yards of the green.

If you want to see your scores improve fast, then spend more time in the short-game area at practice and work on your chipping, pitching, and bunker play. Here are several drills that target these three areas and will help you become more efficient around the greens.

**Umbrella Drill:** Open an umbrella, flip it upside down, and stick it into the ground about 15 feet away from you. Drop a few balls down and try to pitch each one into the umbrella, as if it were a basket, before you move the umbrella back another 15 feet and repeat. Continue pushing the umbrella back to about 60 feet, or 20 yards.

The umbrella gives you a visual target that's often missing in pitching. Most poor pitchers don't think about where they're going to land their ball, nor do they consider the firmness or slope of the green and how much the ball is going to roll out. Players need to calculate where they're going to land the ball and how much it's going to release. This drill helps you to control your landing area better and teaches you what length swing you need to pitch the ball a certain distance. Another thing it does is help you to build a repeatable swing, so you can hit the ball a repeatable distance.

The umbrella serves as a great practice aid. To groove your distance control on short shots, flip it upside down and practice pitching balls into the umbrella from various distances.

**Tee-Square Drill:** Create a three-foot square of tees (see below) about five feet onto the putting surface. Drop a dozen or so balls down in the rough just off the green and practice chipping balls within the square using a variety of different clubs, from your 8-iron to your sand wedge. Just as before, the goal is to see if you can control the distance you fly each ball, which all good chippers are able to do. You'll also get a sense for how much roll each club generates. A sand wedge typically has a carry-to-roll ratio of 1:1, a pitch wedge 1:2, a 9-iron 1:3, and so on. The shorter the distance between you and the hole, the more-lofted club you want to chip with and vice versa.

**One-Handed-Chipping Drill:** Drop a few balls in the rough and hit some chip shots as normal, with one notable exception. As soon as you reach impact, allow your right hand to come off the club (see photo, opposite). This will teach you to lead with the handle through impact, so you can make a descending strike on the ball. Most poor chippers overaccelerate the right hand through impact, so the clubhead passes the handle prematurely. As long as the handle is leaning forward at impact, you should make solid contact and have a consistent, repeatable trajectory.

**The Tee-Square Drill teaches you to land the ball consistently on the green in the same location, so you can better predict the amount of roll it will have.**

**Bunker-Splash Drill:** Draw two parallel lines in the sand about 10 inches apart. Imagine there's a ball midway between each line and take several practice swings, splashing the sand out onto the green. Remember to set up with your shoulders level (feel like your left shoulder is lower than your right) and your weight on your forward leg. See if you can get each divot to start in the same place every time and finish between the lines. The deepest part of the divot should be in the middle, where the ball would be. Most amateurs who struggle from the bunker start their divots too early, behind the line, which leads to skulled and fat shots. Once you're able to make a dollar-bill-sized divot consistently in the right spot, add a ball and repeat. Remember: the object in bunker play is to move the sand and not the ball; the ball is going to travel out on a cushion of sand, in the same direction as the sand.

**By removing your right hand from the club, you'll lead with the handle through impact and hit your chips more precisely.**

**The clubhead should enter the sand on the back line and exit near the front line.**

**Lag-Putting Drill:** Stand in the middle of a practice green and see how close you can putt each ball to the fringe of the green. Mix it up by hitting putts to all four corners of the green (north, south, east, west), so you have a varying amount of uphill, downhill, and sidehill putts and distances. On longer putts, the distance you hit the ball becomes critical, more so than the direction of the putt. This exercise forces you to focus on the speed and distance you hit your putts (because there's no hole), which is the key to avoiding three-putts. It also gives you a feel for the pace and rhythm of the stroke you'll need to lag your putts consistently close to the hole.

**Work on your speed control by putting balls toward all four corners of the practice green. The goal is to hit each putt as close to to the fringe as possible without running the ball into the rough.**

On the range, practice hitting those shots you face most frequently on the course.

## 4. Full-Swing Practice Drills

When you're on the range, practice those shots you hit on a highly repetitive basis. If you frequently find yourself with a 175- to 200-yard approach shot into the green, then practice hitting your hybrid or fairway metal to that yardage. If you're a shorter hitter who can't reach the par-5s in two, then simulate the full wedge shot you're likely to have as your third shot into the green. It doesn't make sense to hit driver after driver on the range because, at most, you should be attempting 14 of these shots during the course of play. Make time for your other clubs, because you might call on them more than your driver.

Here are a few full-swing drills and exercises you can try as well while you're practicing on the range or at home or if you have a few extra minutes on the course.

**Alignment Drill:** Using the tile in your kitchen, foyer, or sidewalk, practice aligning your body properly by setting your feet, knees, hips, and shoulders parallel to the tile lines. Have one of the outside lines be the ball-target line and an inside line be your stance line. The important thing is to get your shoulders as square as possible to your stance line, because your arms tend to follow your shoulders. Players who have their shoulders and chest more open to their target line are prone to slice the ball.

Tiles make for a perfect alignment aid.

**Tee-Path Drill:** Set up a curved gate of tees slightly wider than the width of a 7-iron head, creating a path that curves from the 7 to the 11 on an imaginary clockface. Tee up a ball in the middle of this track and hit the ball with a full range of motion. Generally speaking, to hit a draw you have to swing the clubhead from inside the target line to along the target line to back inside again. If the club is traveling on the correct path, from inside the target line, it has a chance to square up through impact, thus generating more speed, centered contact, and more power.

**Divot Drill:** Draw a straight line along the ground using chalk, a divot repair tool, or a tee. Set up to the line as if a ball were on it and make some swings along the line, carving a divot out on the target side of the line. The divot should take on a rectangular shape, like that of a dollar bill, and start right on the line. After several swings, add a ball and repeat. If you can get the clubhead to bottom out consistently on the target side of the ball, you'll make perfect ball-turf contact with your irons and hit the ball solidly every time.

**The clubhead should travel on a slightly curved arc through impact.**

**A good divot is formed when the clubhead bottoms out on the target side of the ball.**

**Bumper Drill:** Make some slow-motion practice swings with your pitching wedge under the bumper of a golf cart. (A hedge will also suffice.) The bumper will force you to shallow out your swing, on the same inclined angle the club started on at address. If the clubhead approaches the bumper on a steeper angle (too much out to in), it's going to run into the bumper. This drill also forces you to stay down in your posture, because if you raise up out of your spine angle, you'll hit the bumper as well.

**Takeaway Drill:** Set up to a bench so the shaft of your driver rests against the outer edge of the bench. Swing the club back slowly, keeping the shaft in contact with the bench for the first several feet of the backswing. Because the club has an inclined angle to it at address, it will start back on a slightly inclined plane. Many golfers have no concept of what a swing plane is and thus turn or twist the club off its track almost immediately. This drill will teach you how to get the club started back correctly and

**Learn how to shallow out your swing and stay in your posture by making several slow-motion swings under the bumper of a golf cart.**

prevent you from lifting or twisting the club off-plane prematurely. It also helps you see how the club should be delivered back to the ball, which is on the same inclined path.

**Keep the shaft gliding along the edge of the bench for an on-plane takeaway.**

# 5. Stretch Your Body

Before you make any swing changes or ratchet up the intensity of your practice time, get a physical assessment from a physical therapist or golf-specific trainer. Many times, it's your body's physical limitations, and not your swing, that prevent you from getting any better. It could be your body won't allow you to make a full shoulder turn or stay in posture as you swing. An assessment will identify your weaknesses so you can fix them and, in the process, maybe work out a few kinks in your swing.

Golfers should stretch before and after they play to keep their muscles supple and to prevent soreness, especially in the joints, since there is so much rotation in the golf swing. Here are some stretches you can do on the first tee or during your warm-up prior to teeing off. Always make sure to warm up your muscles before you stretch and to stretch your muscles before adding any rotation elements to your exercises. You want to elongate your muscles prior to any kind of rotation movements, such as swinging a golf club.

**Figure-4 Stretch:** Holding onto a golf club for balance (use a longer club, such as a driver), cross your left leg over your right knee and then sit down into your left hip until you feel a good stretch in your left glute muscle. Hold this stretch for about 15 seconds and then repeat on the other side to help stabilize your hip joints and stretch your glutes.

**Hamstring Stretch:** Stand up straight with your feet slightly wider than shoulder width apart and turn your right foot out at a 45-degree angle. Lift the big toe of your right foot off the ground and then bend from your hip joint,

**Figure-4 Stretch**

**Hamstring Stretch**

**Hand-Strengthening Stretch**

toward the elevated toe. Hold for 15 seconds and repeat on the other side to stretch out your hamstrings, so important in maintaining good posture throughout the swing.

**Hand-Strengthening Stretch:** Hold both hands out in front of you with your thumbs up and palms facing each other, so there's some tension in your hands. Curl the joints of your fingers inward, toward your palm, for 20 to 30 reps to work the tendons in your forearms above and below your elbow joints.

**Arm Circles:** Stand straight up with your arms at your sides, palms down and thumbs pointing away from you. Rotate your arms in small circles both forward and backward, 10 times on each side of your shoulder joints. Then rotate your hands so your palms are facing up and your thumbs are pointing behind you (below) and repeat to strengthen your rotator cuff muscles and stabilize your shoulders.

**Arm Circles**

**Shoulder Stretch:** Cross your left arm in front of your chest and place your right arm behind your left forearm, just below the elbow. Pull your left arm farther across your body with your right arm and hold for 15 seconds. No bouncing. Try to keep your left shoulder as far away from your left ear as possible. Repeat with the other arm to help loosen your shoulder joints and make a deeper turn on your backswing.

**Shoulder Stretch**

**Scapular Retraction**

**Left-Handed Swing Drill**

**Scapular-Retraction Exercise:** Hold your arms up at your sides as if you were being told to "stick em up." Pinch your shoulder blades back and down—have the feeling you're trying to put your elbows in your back pockets—and hold for about 15 to 20 seconds. You should feel a stretch across the front of your shoulders, as well as your back. This exercise will help you stabilize the club on the downswing as it's moving away from your body and strengthen your backswing position.

**Left-Handed-Swing Drill:** Take three of the shorter clubs in your bag and swing them 10 to 15 times in each direction—both right-handed and left-handed. Swinging left-handed helps you to stretch out the right side of your body, increasing the range of motion and length to your backswing. It also helps to lengthen the muscles on both sides of your body.

## 6. Fuel Your Body

Look at whatever you're eating or drinking as fuel for your body—what kind of fuel do you want to put in your tank? Walk whenever possible (hiring a caddie will add to your enjoyment of the game) and make sure to drink plenty of water during the course of your round—save the beer and scotch for afterward. Water helps you to focus, which is important later on in the round when your body starts to fatigue. Sports drinks are also okay, but make sure to dilute them with plenty of water and be wary of those that boast too many carbohydrates.

As for foods, fruits (apples, bananas), nuts, trail mixes, granola bars, and all-natural energy bars are all good choices. Again, leave the hot dog and potato chips until after the round. Keep drinking water and munching on healthy snacks and your blood levels will stay fairly normal, allowing you to perform to your peak level for all 18 holes.

## 7. Survey Your Equipment

While the fairways at Pebble Beach appear to be wide open, you have to hit the ball in the right places. If you don't, you can really make life difficult on yourself. If a particular hole doesn't fit your eye, or the landing area is being choked in by some fairway bunkers, then hit your 3-wood. Most amateurs carry a 3-wood in their bag, but they don't look at it as an alternative to their driver. The prospect of losing distance is too great, so they don't even want to consider using another club. But the stronger 3-woods (13-degree models) that many manufacturers offer today are basically 2-woods, so you're really not going to lose all that much distance; chances are, you'll be playing your next shot from the middle of the fairway.

Here are some other things to consider when you're thinking about purchasing some new equipment or modifying your set makeup:

**Replace your long irons.** Ideally, you want to have gaps of about 20 yards between your fairway metals and rescue/hybrid clubs. I advise most of my students to carry no iron longer than a 4- or 5-iron in their bag. The primary reason is because of today's hybrid clubs. These long-iron replacements have a low, deep center of gravity that allows you to launch the ball up in the air fairly easily, something many amateurs struggle to do with a 3- or 4-iron because of their slower swing speeds. The hybrids also have a wider sole on them, which makes them great from the rough and other bad lies.

When choosing your set makeup, look at the percentage of shots you have when you play. What clubs do you use most often? Most amateurs will play a driver and hybrid (or fairway metal) on each hole, especially the longer par-4s and par-5s. Once they get around the green, they tend to hit a wide variety of pitch shots. I would recommend that you put a second hybrid in your bag instead of turning to four wedges—that is, unless you tend to shortside yourself a lot or you're playing a course like Pebble Beach, where you frequently have to pitch the ball over a bunker and stop it quickly. You may want to buy a lob wedge and keep it in the bullpen for such instances, but a wiser choice would be to purchase a 58-degree wedge (between a sand and lob wedge) with a decent amount of bounce to it. A high bounce angle will allow the clubhead to skid through the turf, whereas a lob wedge with little bounce will tend to dig.

**Get a grip.** Replace your grips at least twice a year, preferably before the season and then halfway through. Even if you don't play a lot, the grips tend to pick up perspiration from your hands, plus dirt and moisture from leaving your clubs in your trunk or garage.

**Clean your grooves.** It's very important to keep your grooves fresh, especially on the shorter clubs because they help to channel grass away when it gets between the clubface and the ball. This will help you to generate more spin and control your distances into the greens much better.

**Choose a higher-spinning ball.** Titleist conducted a study a few years ago with two groups of 18-handicap golfers. One group received a ball that they would hit on average 5 to 7 yards farther, and the other group got a ball they would hit 5 to 7 fewer yards. Titleist measured the handicaps of each group at the end of the season, and the players that had the shorter-distance ball actually lowered their handicaps (because they were able to control their short-game shots better); players who had the extra-distance ball saw their handicaps increase.

Don't look at the distance of the ball; look at the spin rate, because that's much more important to the average golfer. Around the green you want a ball that's going to be a little softer and spins more, so it will stop a little faster for you, not to mention have a nicer feel off the putter.

# Jack Nicklaus: Be Good with All of Your Clubs

Most amateurs don't use the practice range as a tune-up for their round; rather, they take the time to work on a swing flaw or two in hopes of correcting it before they tee off. Most pros, however, leave the repair work for after their rounds.

"Once I start playing golf during the season, the practice that I do is more reactive practice," said Jack Nicklaus, who, from 1971 through 1973, finished in the top 10 in 41 of 55 professional events (75 percent). "I react to how I'm playing, how I'm swinging, and the round that I've just played. I get far more done having just finished a round because I know what mistakes I've made and what good things I did. Then I work to try to improve on the good things and figure out why I made those mistakes and how I can eliminate them."

Nicklaus also made it a point to practice with all of his clubs. Too many amateurs today reach right for the driver or easy-to-launch hybrid and skip the clubs they don't like to hit.

"I try not to have a favorite club," said Nicklaus. "I have never had a favorite club in my life. I always felt like I should be equally good with all of them. Maybe I was not always quite as good with my pitching and short game when I was younger. That was probably one of my biggest faults. I knew that my back would not allow me to practice my short game. Bending over on short chips and bunker shots and putting was something that I could never do even from the time I was a kid. My body would allow me to practice my long game. So I felt the better I could develop my long game—and I knew I was a pretty good putter—the easier it would be to avoid and eliminate my weaknesses from my golf game."

The approach shot into the par-5 finishing hole at Pebble Beach.

# Chapter 11

# A Hole-by-Hole Guide to Pebble Beach

Jack Nicklaus said that if he had only one more round to play, he'd choose Pebble Beach Golf Links. He's not alone. Pebble Beach is on many golfers' short lists of courses "they must play before they die." So steeped in history and beauty is this course that hundreds of tourists and golf fans make the pilgrimage out to the 18th hole daily, just to get a glimpse of the famous seaside finishing hole and course they've seen on TV so many times.

So what happens if you get the call to play Pebble Beach? A buddy has a slot for a foursome one Saturday morning and wants you to join him. Of course you're playing! You've been dreaming about walking up the 18th fairway and standing on the same 17th tee where Nicklaus hit his famous 1-iron for years. But your game's not ready. You haven't had one of your best summers, and you're fearful that your dream round won't be so dreamy.

Not to worry. The following hole-by-hole guide will not only prepare you for what you'll face at Pebble Beach, but it will help you shoot your Sunday best. I have played Pebble Beach as both a caddie and an instructor hundreds

of times, with golfers of all different skills. I've seen the best players in the world attack these holes through four U.S. Opens and countless Crosby and AT&T Pebble Beach National Pro-Ams; I've also seen many golfers make a mess of these holes.

Whether you're a single-digit handicapper who is looking to shoot around par, a mid-handicapper seeking to break 90, or a high handicapper just hoping to look respectable, the following guide to playing Pebble Beach will help you accomplish your goal. It will be like having a professional caddie on your bag. Most importantly, it will allow you to have the time of your life, because ultimately, no matter how breathtaking the scenery, you want to play your best golf. If you play well, the experience will be that much greater.

And for those of you not lucky enough to play Pebble Beach—at least not yet—there are tips in this chapter that transfer well to any course you play. Regardless of your handicap, your course management skills and scores will improve by reading this chapter.

**Note:** So that everyone can walk away from each hole with his or her target score, I've broken each hole into three strategic categories: 1) how to make birdie, 2) how to make par, and 3) how to make bogey. The birdie tips are for your 0- to 9-handicapper, playing from the blue tees; the par tips for the 10- to 19-handicapper, playing from the golds; and the bogey tips for the 20-and-higher handicapper, playing from the whites. Refer to Chapter 2 to see which tees you should play.

## Hole 1, Par-4

Blue Tees: 377 Yards; Gold: 346; White: 332

**How to make birdie:** Hit your tee shot as far up the fairway as you can, to the first bunker on the left. Favor the left-center fairway off the tee because, that far up, the ball tends to bounce to the right more. On your approach shot, you have to challenge the flagstick, but you also want to make sure to leave the ball below the hole so you have an uphill putt at birdie.

**How to make par:** Hit your 200-yard club off the tee to the widest part of the fairway. The approach shot plays uphill, and the ball tends to curve to the right—because the fairway slopes from left to right—so take one extra club and swing easy. If you miss short, that's okay; the one thing you don't want to do on this hole is hit your approach into the right greenside bunker, which is easy to do.

**How to make bogey:** It's the first hole on the course, so you want to walk into it easy. Off the tee, hit a hybrid or fairway wood about 180 yards to the corner of the dogleg. From here, you want to hit a 125-yard shot, which will leave you 30 yards short of the greenside bunkers. Don't make the mistake of hitting too much club on your second shot, because you don't want to be in the greenside bunkers or pitching over them.

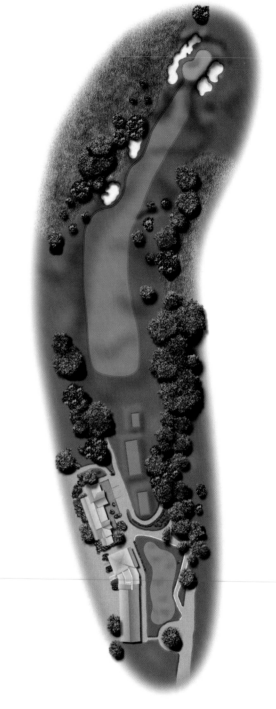

## Hole 2, Par-5

Blue Tees: 511 Yards; Gold: 460; White: 428

**Birdie:** Like the first hole, the fairway slopes from left to right, so hit your tee shot at the middle of the left fairway bunker to allow the ball to feed into the center of the fairway. For your second shot, you should have about 220 yards to a narrow green well protected by bunkers, so choose a club you can hit high and soft. If you miss the green, the easiest shot you're going to have is from the right greenside bunker because you'll be blasting out into an uphill green. Miss the green left, and you have little chance of getting the ball up and down.

**Par:** Aim at the left edge of the left fairway bunker and let your tee shot bleed to the right. To clear the cross-bunker, which is about 75 yards short of the green, you need to carry your second shot about 170–180 yards. If you have a nice, clean lie then go for it, but, if not, play it as a three-shot hole and lay up short of the cross-bunker. That will leave you with about 110 yards in for your third shot. Take the cautious approach: you're just getting started on the course, so you don't want to make a big number right away by hitting your ball into the cross-bunker or out of bounds.

**Bogey:** This hole is scary for the bogey golfer, not just because of the cross-bunker but also because of the two large bunkers on either side of the green. If you're not confident in your bunker game or about pitching the ball up and over a bunker, then lay up on your third shot just short of the green and chip on. A warning about your second shot on this hole and all lay-up shots: most golfers don't lay up to a precise yardage, as they do when playing to the flagstick. Make sure you have a target in mind

(one of the many trees bordering the cross-bunker would be a good aiming spot on No. 2) and hit one less club so you know the ball won't get there. By taking less club, you'll be able to make an aggressive, confident swing toward your target, thus keeping the ball in play.

# Hole 3, Par-4

Blue Tees: 390 Yards; Gold: 374; White: 334

**Birdie:** A sweeping draw around the corner will give you the best opportunity at birdie. Your starting line is the right edge of the kidney-shaped bunker closest to the fairway. Start the ball on this line and bend it about 20 yards to the left, and you should have 100 yards or less in for your second shot. The L-shaped green is the firmest on the course and is surrounded by trouble, so it's critical you hit the ball the correct distance.

**Par:** The raised, kidney-shaped bunker right in your line of sight hides much of the fairway and makes the landing area seem much farther away than it is. A marker on the tee will tell you how far it is to cover this bunker (170 yards), but you must fit your tee shot between the bunker and a new set of fairway bunkers ready to catch any tee ball that runs through the fairway. A 220-yard shot (3-wood) is a good, safe option. Your job on your second shot is to put the ball in the middle of the green, two-putt, and move onto the 4th hole. Anywhere on the green is going to leave you with a fairly short putt, but long is dead, and neither greenside bunker shot is an easy up and down.

**Bogey:** Don't challenge the corner of this dogleg; play your tee shot straight or a little out to the right. This will leave you with a long approach shot (150–175 yards), but that's okay, as you want to chunk the distance on your second shot anyway, laying up to the bottom of the hill. The green here is too small to hold with a long club, and if you hit into any one of those greenside bunkers, you're in deep trouble.

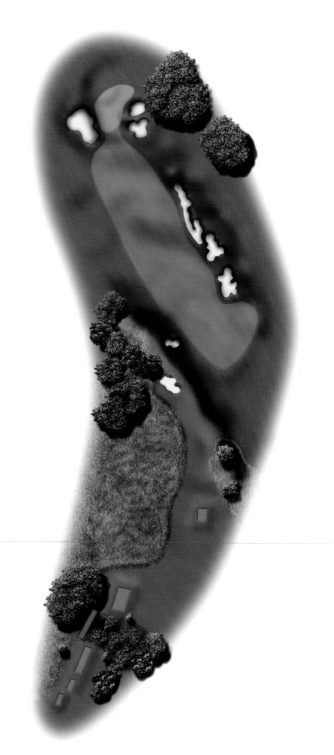

# Hole 4, Par-4

Blue Tees: 326 Yards; Gold: 307; White: 295

**Birdie:** The shortest par-4 on the course requires a tee shot of about 250 yards uphill to cover two fairway bunkers recently pinched in toward the ocean. Be careful approaching the green because the ball tends to spin a lot. The green slopes significantly from back to front, so it's best to be below the hole, where you have an uphill putt at birdie. If you leave your approach shot pin high, your putt could break as much as five feet.

**Par:** A 180- to 200-yard tee shot to the fattest part of the fairway will leave just over 100 yards to the green. From there, try to put the ball on the front of the green, below the flagstick. Look over to the boats in Stillwater Cove to see which way the bows are pointing, as this will tell you which direction the wind is blowing. The bow, or front of the boat, always points into the wind.

**Bogey:** If your tendency is to slice, tee the ball up on the far right-hand side of the box and aim away from the ocean, toward the pot bunker. With your slice/fade, you should be able to find the fairway. If you lose your tee shot to the ocean, don't sweat it because the right side is played as a lateral hazard; you can still make bogey. Your approach shot is uphill, so play one more club than you think is necessary and take dead aim at the front of the green. Favor the right greenside bunker because the one on the left has a higher lip, and the green runs away from you, toward the ocean.

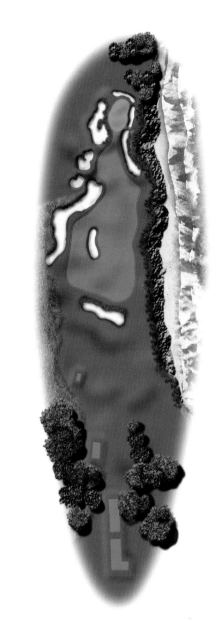

The par-4 4th hole.

# Hole 5, Par-3

Blue Tees: 192 Yards; Gold: 142; White: 130

**Birdie:** The safe play is to the left-center of the green. Start your ball at the left greenside bunker, which is actually in the middle of the green, and let it drift to the right. The green slopes from left to right, but there's not as much slope as there appears, so your tee shot should hold. If you miss, make your mistake short and left so you can chip or putt the ball onto the green. Par is a great score on this hole; birdie is a bonus.

**Par:** Take the same line at the left greenside bunker off the tee. If you have trouble fading the ball, make sure to hit a club that will get you to the middle of the green but no farther. If you go any longer, you risk hitting into the aforementioned bunker, which is a difficult up and down.

**Bogey:** Negotiating yourself around the two greenside bunkers is pivotal to making bogey. Do not flirt with the flagstick, which is usually behind the massive greenside bunker on the right-hand side. Short and left is okay; in fact, if you can place your tee shot on the front-left portion of the green or close to it, you can make a run at par.

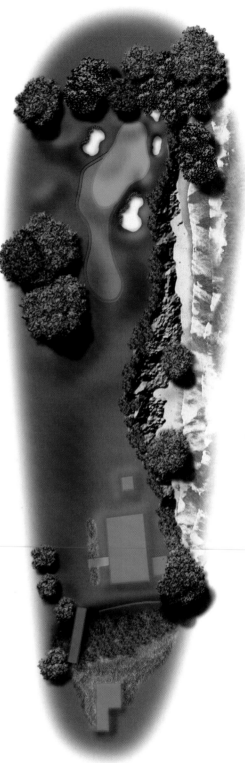

The par-3 5<sup>th</sup> hole.

# Hole 6, Par-5

Blue Tees: 506 Yards; Gold: 487; White: 467

**Birdie:** The fairway bunkers on the left have been moved forward and closer to the coastline, bringing the ocean more into play. As a result, the longer hitters will have to challenge the right side of the fairway and hit a draw, since the fairway slopes from left to right. A good drive will leave you with a blind second shot of about 230 yards. As you're walking toward your ball, stop about 30 yards short of the fairway bunkers on the left, as this will give you a line (the lollipop tree behind the green) into the green. The closer you get to the hill, the harder it is to visualize a line.

**Par:** Take a more conservative approach off the tee and lay up short of the fairway bunkers; if you hit into the bunkers, you're going to have a hard time reaching the top of the hill. To reach the upper fairway, you're going to need to advance your second shot about 175–185 yards. That will leave you with a full wedge to a green that's very open up front.

**Bogey:** Lay up short of the bunkers with a hybrid or fairway wood and then chunk your distance to the bottom of the hill. This should leave you with about 180 yards to the green. Hit a short iron to the top of the hill and then pitch on. If you hit a good tee shot and want to get on top of the hill, aim left toward the 8th fairway.

The par-5 6th hole.

# Hole 7, Par-3

Blue Tees: 109 Yards; Gold: 98; White: 94

**Birdie:** If there's no wind, play to the front yardage (92 yards to the front-left portion of the green), which should leave you in the middle of the green. Keep your head down and no peeking! Place trust in your yardage and make a confident swing.

**Par:** Assuming no wind, play it like you would an 80-yard shot. Make sure your sand or gap wedge can cover that distance. Many golfers overestimate how far they hit their wedges and either come up short or swing so hard that they pull their shot to the left. You might be better off taking a pitching wedge, choking down on it, and making a smooth, three-quarter-length swing.

**Bogey:** Forget about the flagstick—anywhere on the green is a victory and a photo op. Make your last look to the right side of the green because when playing shots downhill, the tendency is to look left; the ocean to the right will also have you aiming left. You don't want to visit the left greenside bunker because the lip is fairly high and there's little green to hit to; the front bunker is the easiest to escape because it slopes upward, and the green is a much bigger target.

The par-3 7th hole.

# Hole 8, Par-4

Blue Tees: 427 Yards; Gold: 400; White: 373

**Birdie:** On the tee, aim for the dome-shaped window on the Firestone house (see photo on page 23) and hit your 230-yard club. Although the green sits well below the fairway, it doesn't play considerably downhill—maybe five yards less. Hit your approach shot on a line between the gloved bunker short and left of the green and the flagstick. You'd rather make a mistake short because the opening to the green is large, and it plays uphill, leaving a fairly easy pitch.

**Par:** You want your tee shot to finish in line with the dome-shaped window on the Firestone house. If your tendency is to fade the ball, start your tee shot to the left side of the house so it finishes in line with the dome-shaped window and vice versa for a draw. A 220-yard drive will leave you with approximately 170–180 yards to the green. Aim at the glove-shaped bunker and make as free a swing as you can, making sure to brush the turf just ahead of the ball.

**Bogey:** Choose your 180- to 200-yard club off the tee and take aim at the fence sitting just below the yellow house in the distance. The farther left you are off the tee, the less ocean you have to carry. Play your next shot (a short iron) toward the glove-shaped bunker on the left. The ball should hit and trickle to the right, leaving you with a relatively easy wedge shot from the lower fairway. Don't flirt with the ocean on this hole; left is your friend.

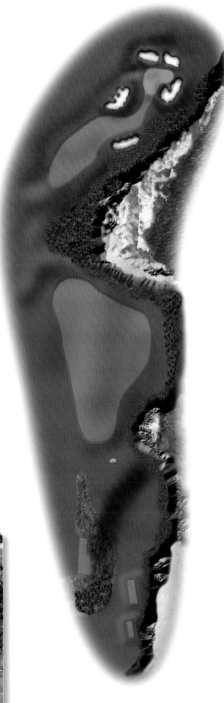

The par-4 8th hole.

# Hole 9, Par-4

Blue Tees: 481 Yards; Gold: 460; White: 435

**Birdie:** Aim a little right of the fairway bunker on the left and swing away. The ball should run partially down the slope, leaving you with about 180 to 200 yards. Now you've got to hit your iron shot of the day. The ball is going to be below your feet, so it will come out on a lower, flatter trajectory and may drift a little to the right. Aim left at the deep-bunkered gully because the ocean is very tight to the right side of the green and closer than most people think.

**Par:** Downhill, sidehill lie, ocean right, small, narrow green...it's wise to hit your second shot short of the deep-bunkered gully on the left, leaving yourself with a flat lie and a full spinning wedge into the green. The closer you get to the bunker on your second shot, the softer pitch you'll have into the green.

**Bogey:** There's more room to the right than you think off the tee, so go ahead and hit driver. Again, lay up short of the deep bunker on the left; you don't want to be in there. Try to place your third shot in the center or right-center of the green, below the flagstick, to give yourself a look at an uphill or right-to-left breaking putt.

# Hole 10, Par-4

Blue Tees: 441 Yards; Gold: 429; White: 409

**Birdie:** Tee your ball up on the far right side of the tee box and aim at the middle of the large fairway bunker on the left. The ball will be below your feet on your second shot and will tend to move toward the ocean, so make sure to aim far enough left of the green (at the left greenside bunker) to allow the ball to drift 10 to 15 yards to the right. If you start the ball at the middle of the green and it drifts at all, you'll be in the ocean.

**Par:** Again, aim away from the ocean on your tee shot. Be careful on your second shot because sometimes with a hanging lie, the ball doesn't curve to the right. It's very easy to lose your balance and pull the shot to the left, so take one extra club and swing in balance. The green sits more to the right, closer to the ocean than it does on No. 9, so make sure you borrow enough room to the left.

**Bogey:** Play it as a three-shot hole. On the third shot, make sure to aim at the left greenside bunker to allow the ball to curve to the right. If you're still worried about the ocean, go left of the bunker, where you'll be left with a short, pin-high pitch from very manageable rough.

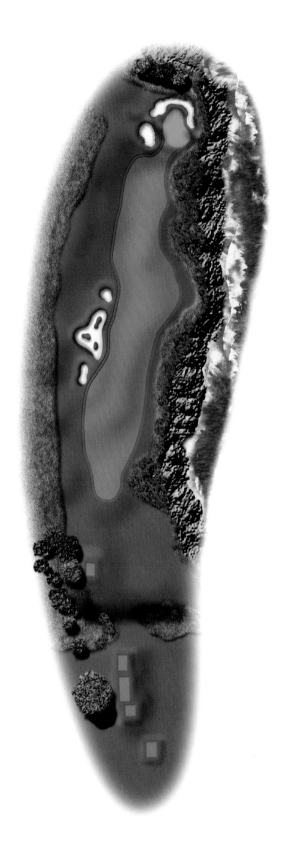

# Hole 11, Par-4

Blue Tees: 373 Yards; Gold: 349; White: 340

**Birdie:** Aim at the telephone pole in the distance and let it fly. The hole plays considerably uphill (one look behind you will give you an indication how much), so take one more club than normal on your approach but be careful not to overclub. You're much better off being short of the flagstick than above the hole, which is extremely slick. Because the green plays uphill, the ball will tend to grab a little and stop, which should help your cause.

**Par:** Just as above, aim at the telephone pole and favor the left side of the fairway, which gives you the best angle into the green. Add about five yards to your second shot for the hill, but make sure you stay below the hole. If you come up a little short of the green, that's fine; you can still get your ball up and down for par.

**Bogey:** There's a cross-bunker (on the right) that looks to be right next to the green but is actually 50 yards short of it. This is a good target for your second shot because you want to lay up left of this bunker. From this position, you'll have a fairly straightforward uphill pitch to a wide-open green.

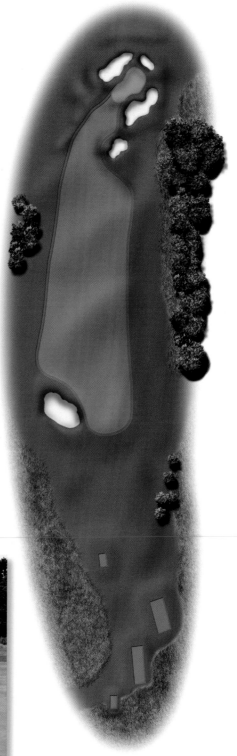

The par-4 11th hole.

# Hole 12, Par-3

Blue Tees: 201 Yards; Gold: 187; White: 179

**Birdie:** The green is wide, but not very deep, so you need to hit the ball the correct distance to give yourself a putt at birdie. The hole does play downhill some, but you want to play to the yardage on the scorecard. Check the wind by looking to the tops of the trees and back to the flag on No. 11, because it's very hard to detect. Typically, this tee shot plays into the wind.

**Par:** Anywhere on the green is a good shot, so forget about playing to the flagstick. Again, club selection is critical; play to the yardage on the scorecard but make sure to gauge the wind beforehand so you're not left wondering why your tee shot came up short in the bunker.

**Bogey:** There's not much room to bail out on this hole, so your best bet is to lay up short of the green between the two bunkers and pitch the ball on. This is a challenging pitch for the average golfer because of the tight lie. Favor your sand wedge over your lob wedge because it has more bounce to it and is less likely to dig. The ball may come out a little lower, but it will have more spin and stopping power.

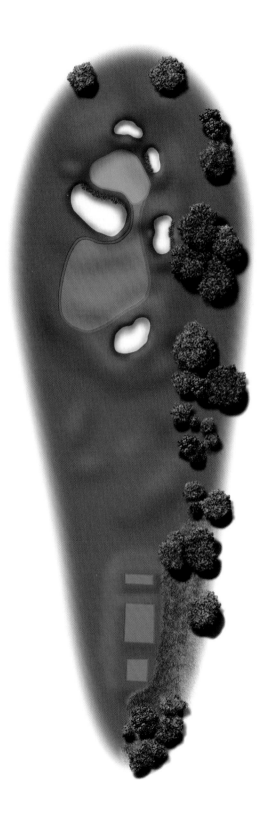

# Hole 13, Par-4

Blue Tees: 403 Yards; Gold: 391; White: 372

**Birdie:** Aim at the two palm trees behind the green and let the shaft out. This should put you in the left-center of the fairway. The second shot plays uphill and into the wind from a hook lie, so it's best to keep the ball low, where you'll have some control over it. The green is severely sloped from right to left, so keep your approach shot below the hole; anything long or to the right is likely to result in a bogey.

**Par:** On your second shot, grip down on the club to help keep the ball down, below the wind. Be careful not to overshoot the green to the left, as you'll be left with a blind uphill, sidehill pitch to a green 10 feet above you.

**Bogey:** Hit driver at the two palm trees and then lay up short of the green, left of the two large bunkers farthest from the green. These two bunkers are far enough from the green to give even the most-skilled golfers trouble. This is an easy hole to make double bogey on without even thinking. Leave yourself an uphill chip or pitch for your third shot, and you might just walk away with par.

# Hole 14, Par-5

Blue Tees: 572 Yards; Gold: 560; White: 548

**Birdie:** Forget about going for this green in two. Aim at the eucalyptus trees in the distance (toward the gold tees on No. 6) and let it fly. You then need to advance your second shot as far as you can up the fairway to have a scoring club into the green. The third shot plays about 15 yards extra uphill, so choose one more club and aim at the right side of the giant bunker fronting the green. Make sure you have enough club to get the ball up on top of the green; anything short will roll down the slope, leaving you with a tricky pitch. Favor the right side of the green on your approach shot.

**Par:** Advance your second shot as far as you can, which should leave you with an approach in the vicinity of 140 yards. Aim at the right-hand side of the green and knock it up there as far as you can. Don't worry about being long because there's a little backstop that will stop the ball and shove it toward the flag if it's up on top.

**Bogey:** Play it as a four-shot hole and be careful not to leave your third shot short and left of the mammoth greenside bunker. You want to approach the green from the right side of the fairway, which opens up the right side of the green and keeps you a safe distance from the bunker.

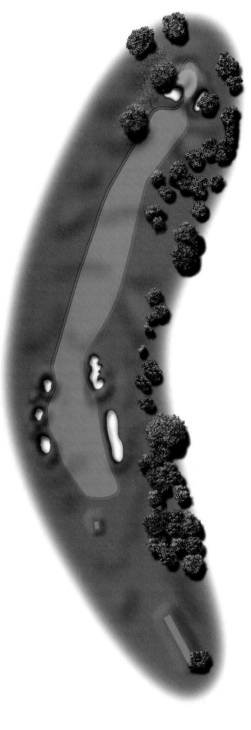

**The par-5 14th hole.**

# Hole 15, Par-4

Blue Tees: 396 Yards; Gold: 377; White: 340

**Birdie:** Hit your driver directly at the right greenside bunker to avoid the pot bunker on the left, 100 yards from the green. Like many of the holes at Pebble Beach, you're much better off being below the hole than above it. The green appears flat, but if you don't see any break, factor in the ocean to your left, as putts at Pebble Beach tend to break toward it.

**Par:** The tee box points you well right, toward the road, which is out of bounds. Use the left edge of the white tee box to align yourself more left and hit your 3-wood; the shot plays downhill, and you'll pick up a lot of yardage on the ground. Your approach shot will appear more downhill than it actually is, so play to the yardage.

**Bogey:** Hit your fairway wood or hybrid off the tee. Your first priority is to put the ball in play, not on 17-Mile Drive. Hit the fairway, and you've got a green-light special: if you're playing well, go for green; if not, try to cover the heart-shaped bunker 50 yards short and right of the green and pitch on.

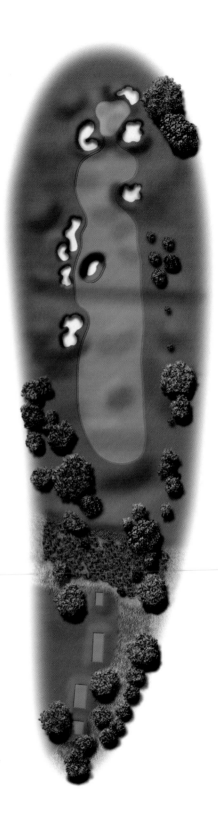

# Hole 16, Par-4

Blue Tees: 401 Yards; Gold: 376; White: 368

**Birdie:** Give your driver a rest and knock a 3-wood out there over the large island bunker in the center of the fairway. That should leave you with a fairly flat lie and a downhill view of the green from 120 to 150 yards. The farther you hit your drive, the more downhill the second shot becomes. The green slopes considerably from right to left, so stay below the flagstick at all costs.

**Par:** Be wary of the pot bunker, which pinches in the right side of the fairway about 235 yards from the tee. The second shot plays almost a full club less because of the elevation change. Choose wisely and keep your approach shot below the hole; anything right of the green brings bogey into the equation.

**Bogey:** Aim at the left edge of the large island bunker off the tee. On your second shot, lay up to the bottom of the fairway, short of the big cross-bunker. From there, you'll have a manageable wedge shot of about 75–80 yards. Be careful not to lay up too far left or right, or you risk getting blocked out by the trees.

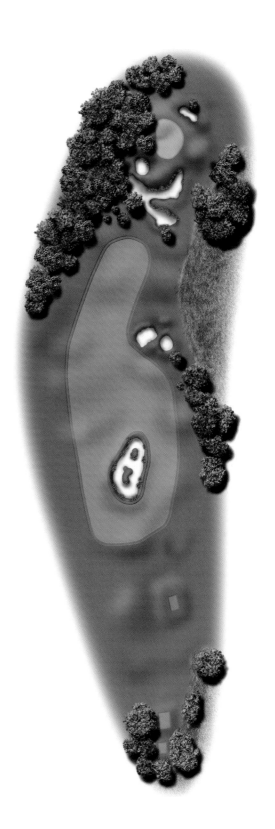

# Hole 17, Par-3

Blue Tees: 177 Yards; Gold: 170; White: 163

**Birdie:** As you approach the tee, make sure to stop on the championship tee (behind the 4th tee) to see where Jack Nicklaus hit his famous 1-iron at the 1972 U.S. Open. You won't need to hit a 1-iron here, but it will take a magnificent iron shot or a well-placed flagstick (to stop your ball) to make birdie. The green is a figure eight on its side, so there's very little space to fit your ball. Check out the temperature and environment before you tee it up: if it's cool, the ball isn't going to carry as far, so you may want to take one more club. The flag on top of The Beach Club will tell you the wind's direction.

**Par:** Take dead aim at the flag. Why not? Magic can happen at any time, and besides, how often will you be in this position again? If you miss short, you'll have a relatively easy bunker shot. If you have a great round going and you're not confident in your ability to hit the ball the perfect distance, play your tee shot off to the right and leave yourself a putt or chip across the green. This is a strategy many players use during the U.S. Open, when the pin is tucked left.

**Bogey:** If you're feeling good, go for it; if not, aim at the small patch of fairway short and right of the green and play it as a four-shot hole. Don't be timid on your second shot and make sure to take a high line with your chip or pitch.

**The par-3 17th hole.**

# Hole 18, Par-5

Blue Tees: 543 Yards; Gold: 532; White: 509

**Birdie:** The key is to be left of the two trees in the right-center of the fairway, so you don't have to negotiate them on your second shot and can advance the ball as far as possible. The first tree is 280 yards from the tee, so it requires a pretty good poke. The better players will chase a 3-wood up the fairway as close to the green as possible for their second shot, sometimes pushing it up into the front greenside bunker. This leaves them with a short pitch or relatively simple bunker shot. If you have less than 60 yards in for your third shot, you have a strong chance at making birdie.

**Par:** Hit 3-wood short of the two trees in the center of the fairway. From here, it essentially becomes a short, 300-yard par-4. Advance your next shot about 180 yards to the right elbow of the fairway, to give yourself a good angle in for your approach shot. Look to the flags on top of The Lodge (and chiminey smoke) to see which way the wind is blowing before you play your next shot. The third shot plays a little uphill, so take an extra club.

**Bogey:** Choose whichever club you feel will keep you in play off the tee, then advance your next shot 150 to 175 yards so you're in line with the back edge of the long, sea wall bunker. You should be able to get home from here; if you're not in position to reach the green, then lay up short of the large overhanging tree and frontal bunker and pitch on.

*Hole illustrations by Tim Cottrill, provided courtesy of MillerBrown.*

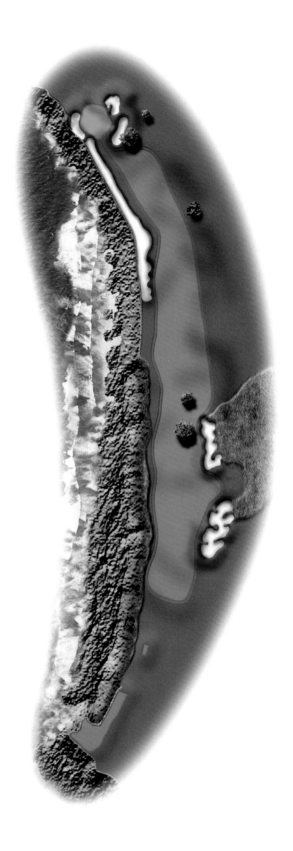

# Afterword

**W**e often use the term *golf instructor* to define the relationship between you and the person working to provide you with the fundamentals necessary to enjoy golf—the greatest game ever played.

In my experience, there are people who *instruct*, and then there are those, as rare as priceless gemstones, we call *teachers. Instructor* suggests mechanical, disciplined, specific, and controlling, but *teacher* makes us consider far more than just the question of a fundamentally balanced golf swing.

My friend, Laird Small, is in every way the consummate teacher… and why? Because he blends a love of the game with a remarkable background and most important—far more important than any other quality—the heart that always places his students first and never, ever has him looking at his watch reminding you that your one-hour lesson is up. Laird teaches with his mind, soul, heart, and body, and it's what makes him different from all of the instructors who have tried to make Tom Sullivan, blind golfer, a player.

There have been maybe 50 blind golfers who have worked to enjoy the game since World War II. Until I came along, all of them had been people who learned the game as sighted golfers—many with low handicaps. So, Laird was presented with the problem of trying to create verbal pictures and physical exercises that could allow me to understand the complexity of movement that has no absolutes.

I think it was Arnold Palmer who said that the only commonality in the golf swing is the six inches before impact and the six inches following it, and from what I've heard, there are as many different techniques as there are players on the PGA TOUR. People talk about one- and two-plane golf swings, stack and tilt, limited hip turns, and big-time shoulder turns that create an X-factor; hands active, hands passive, turn versus slide, and on and on.

A sighted player disseminates this information visually and decides what works for him, but when you're blind it can only occur through specific feel and the trust you establish in whom? The teacher. Laird has done everything possible to make me a player. Once, he created and wore a jacket made out of cellophane so I could hear the rhythm of his swing. There was a metronome on the putting green. Then there was the torture device I wore around my waist with two sticks that clicked together when my arms fell in the slot. He gave me a weight on a string to teach me to feel centrifugal and centripetal force as the weight moved through space. Then there was a complex swing aid that I'd stand inside with the club moving on an arc specific to my height and arm length. But these were only devices. The enthusiasm, the intense thought process, the patience, the communication, the complete engagement, and the love for the game in his student—that's what came from the soul of Laird Small, my teacher.

It was raining one day in Pebble Beach, the same kind of rain you experience on the west coast of Ireland and Scotland—that straight-down pelting rain driven by the winds blowing off the sea—and there I was, buffeted by the storm but supported by my teacher, working on my swing. Laird could have easily canceled the lesson, but I had arrived from Los Angeles, and we had planned our time together for two months. Remember how I told you he doesn't use a watch? Well, my lesson was supposed to be an hour, and it wasn't even three. After four hours I couldn't lift my arms anymore, and he was still suggesting that now might be the ideal time to putt because I would be in a very relaxed state. You're crazy, my friend. I was exhausted, and what were you doing? Still teaching with every fiber of your being.

So, as you read this book, know that it is written with the wisdom that has made Laird Small a PGA Teacher of the Year, with knowledge gained through hundreds of clinics, seminars, and lessons given at beautiful Pebble Beach. It is written with instincts that make my friend that rarest of all diamonds, a teacher providing his best gift to every student he encounters on the practice tee and every person who will enjoy these pages.

—Tom Sullivan
Blind actor, singer, author, motivational